THE REGIONAL ITALIAN COOKBOOK

THE REGIONAL ITALIAN COOKBOOK

Recipes from
The Silver Spoon

North

Piedmont
19

Valle d'Aosta
35

Liguria
49

Lombardy
63

Trentino-Alto Adige
77

Veneto
93

Friuli-Venezia Giulia
111

Emilia-Romagna
127

Center

Tuscany
147

Marche
163

Umbria
175

Lazio
189

South

Abruzzo
207

Molise
221

Campania
237

Basilicata
255

Puglia
269

Calabria
283

Islands

Sicily
301

Sardinia
319

Legends

Vegetarian	
Vegan	
Gluten-free	
Dairy-free	
Nut-free	
5 ingredients or fewer	

Foreword

Italian cuisine is a rich tapestry of regional specialties, each telling a story shaped by local history, culture, and ingredients. This collection of regional Italian recipes, brought to you by The Silver Spoon, highlights the diverse culinary traditions found across Italy, from the north's hearty Alpine dishes to the south's vibrant coastal recipes.

Since its inception, The Silver Spoon has been a trusted guide in Italian cooking, showcasing the importance of regional recipes in preserving Italy's culinary heritage. This book serves as an essential resource for anyone looking to explore authentic Italian cuisine, offering a wide range of recipes that are rooted in tradition yet inviting for home cooks.

Italian food embodies community and family. Meals are often a gathering of loved ones, filled with warmth, laughter, and shared experiences. The recipes in this book not only reflect the flavors of each region but also emphasize the joy of cooking and sharing meals together. Each dish encapsulates local ingredients and techniques, allowing you to appreciate the richness of Italian culture through its food.

In this collection, you will find easy-to-follow recipes that encourage experimentation while respecting traditional methods. From pasta dishes drenched in rich sauces to simple, fresh salads bursting with flavor, every recipe is designed to inspire you to cook with confidence and creativity.

Embrace the variety that Italian cuisine offers. Let this book guide you through the unique tastes of each region, reminding you that cooking is not just about the result but the journey of bringing people together.

Buon appetito!

Introduction

The flavors of Italy

Pasta, cold meats, cheeses, vegetables, and fruits galore. Italy has extraordinary, internationally recognized produce and food products that have made its cuisine both an undisputed delicacy and a nutritional asset.

ITALY IS PASTA

Italy is the master at producing, cooking, and flavoring pasta. There are over 150 different varieties, short and long, that cook to "al dente" perfection, and hundreds of sauces and flavor combinations to match. But spaghetti has always been the country's most warmly welcomed ambassador around the world. Already by the mid-1800s, Gragnano, Torre Annunziata, Amalfi, and Naples, all in Campania, had become major centers for pasta-making, with pasta factories and noisy streets filled with macaroni, and where spaghetti would be stretched out on open looms to dry by the heat of the sun. Later, as the industry developed, other important regions emerged, such as Emilia-Romagna, Abruzzo, Puglia, and Sicily. Today, Italy has an annual pasta production of three million tons, half of which is for export, while each of the country's inhabitants consumes about sixty-two pounds (twenty-eight kilograms) of it each year. Added to this are the amounts of fresh and filled pastas that are also part of its DNA: tortellini in Bologna, cappelletti in Reggio Emilia, cappellacci in Ferrara, cannelloni in Rome, and all over Italy you can find much-loved lasagna and countless varieties of ravioli, with the added value of bringing the whole family together at mealtimes, even today.

ITALY IS A MOUNTAIN OF CURED MEATS

Italy leads the world in the art of transforming the meat of the beloved pig into an amazing array of products. Emilia-Romagna is as close as you will come to pork paradise, with cities and towns even identified with particular products: Zibello, for example, is known for culatello and Felino salami; Bologna for mortadella; and Parma for its namesake ham (on average, every Parma resident consumes six hams a year), a rosy, sweet, and delicate prosciutto branded with the five-pointed ducal crown, and the first in Italy to enjoy protected designation of origin (PDO) status: its production is restricted to the province of Parma (bordered to the north by the Via Emilia and to the south by the Enza river), which rises to an altitude of 2,953 feet (900 meters) and where the air is ideal for curing. However, Italy is dotted with other splendid ham-producing locations. They include the Berici and Euganean Hills of Veneto, whose excellent prosciutto bears the winged lion of Venice. And then there is San Daniele in Friuli: 2.5 million hams a year, which are immediately recognized because they keep their feet (trotters). Even higher up, at an altitude of 3,937 feet (1,200 meters), Carnia is undoubtedly Italy's highest ham-producing center and home to smoked Sauris prosciutto. Moving down toward central Italy we come to the region of Montefeltro, where, nestled in the Natural Regional Park of Sasso Simone and Simoncello, the village of Carpegna is home to two exceptional hams, with production deliberately restricted to 150,000 pieces per year, such is the care taken in their expert curing: soft and sweet San Leo prosciutto (the most expensive ham in Italy) and La Ghianda prosciutto, flavored with black pepper and juniper. Other notable cured hams are produced in Marche, Tuscany, and Sicily.

ITALY IS HEAVEN FOR CHEESE-LOVERS

From the north to the south, Italy's regions produce such an abundant supply of milk that cheese has always been made, either by natural methods in the past or with the industrial processes of the present. Italy is home to more than four hundred cheeses, practically all of them exceptional in terms of their diversity of flavors and levels of aging and hardness. Famous throughout the world is Parmesan cheese, Parmigiano Reggiano, centuries-old goodness that the whole world envies the Italians for and (unfortunately) copies. Then there is Pecorino Romano, with its sweet "bite" that enlivens the palate. White, smooth, and shiny mozzarella di bufala is the only "genuine" buffalo-milk mozzarella; anyone traveling to discover the south of the country knows that after the twists and turns of the coast, descending toward the lowlands of the Piana del Sele, you enter its realm: Battipaglia, Eboli, Capaccio, Benevento, Caserta, Naples, and Salerno. Other delicacies include provolone from Puglia, a stretch-curd cheese "spun" by expert hands to a harmonious score of spicy and delicate notes; Taleggio from Lombardy, its softness being its sign of excellence; the seductive Gorgonzola from the province of Novara, made using an intriguing ferment of divine green mold; white fontina from the Valle d'Aosta that is made into a creamy and indulgent fondue; and fresh white ricotta cheeses to spread on bread, the intense flavor of its smoked or baked versions grated over pasta.

ITALY IS THE FRAGRANCE OF EXCELLENT OILS

Oils from Tuscany, strong flavored and fragrant like those from Chianti, or pale and delicate like those from Lucca, all have a taste as intact as the landscape, of the vines and olive trees of their origin. The green and lightly flavored oil of Umbria is scarce, making it highly prized, the undisputed condiment of a cuisine that still ignores the gentle flattery of butter. On the other hand, almonds and pine nuts are the flavor of the very fine olive oil from Liguria, with its golden color and subtle fruity aroma—the star, together with basil, of that marvelous green sauce called pesto, one of the absolute hallmarks of Italian cuisine.

ITALY IS A PARADISE OF VEGETABLE GARDENS AND ORCHARDS

Eggplants (aubergines); zucchini (courgettes); fennel; tomatoes; peppers; artichokes of not just one type, but of the most varied shapes, colors, and flavors; dozens of crisp lettuces, long and round varieties of radicchio, and curls of puntarelle; the scent of basil and mint, and the aroma of truffles. Italy is also a fortunate land of rare and sought-after flavors. Like the basil that was once grown on the sloping terraces of the legendary stretch of coastline between Pegli and Pra and is now produced in greenhouses. Like the truffle from Alba, in the Langhe area of Piedmont, pale shavings of which form a thick layer on fondues, taglierini (*tajarin*), and carpaccio. In the north of the Marche region, the white truffles found in Acqualagna, Sant'angelo in Vado and Visso are overwhelmingly in demand. In neighboring Umbria, the lumpiest and most fragrant of all is the "fine black truffle," which is sprinkled into skillets (frying pans) and enveloped in fluffy omelets. And then there is the smell of pears and melons, the fragrance of peaches and apricots, of cherries, strawberries, and raspberries. Of oranges, lemons, and mandarins, which are not only seen as fruit with a hundred different sweet and sour flavors, but also turned into incredible salads enhanced with oil and seasoned with salt crystals. Moreover, Sicily is truly a paradise for citrus fruits, which ripen in the warm sun of this most prolific land.

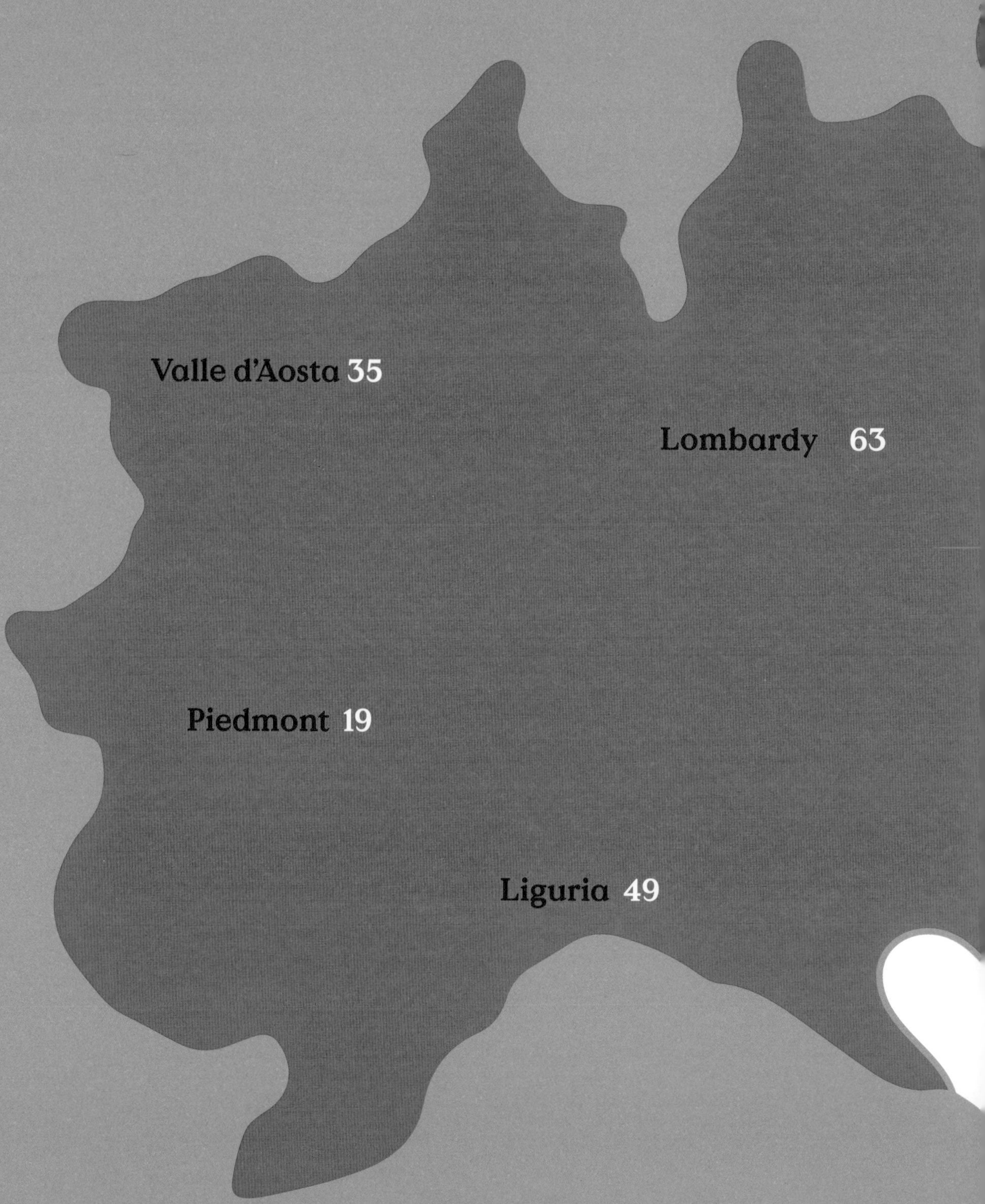
Valle d'Aosta 35
Lombardy 63
Piedmont 19
Liguria 49

North

Trentino-Alto Adige **77**

Friuli-Venezia Giulia **111**

Veneto **93**

Emilia-Romagna **127**

Piedmont

Wine, cheese, and truffles

Piedmont, filled with the scent of vineyards, woods, and the countryside, is to be savored. It is where the magnificent culinary treasures of small towns raise them to the rank of "capitals." Examples include Castelmagno, home to the legendary cheese; Alba, with its precious white truffle and Barolo, the king of wines; and Asti, with its fleshy square peppers and magnificent Moscato wine. It is a region full of signature dishes, from vitel tonné (page 26) to bollito misto (page 30) and bonet al caffé (page 32). It is where the most ordinary menu reads: taglierini (*tajarin*) with butter and truffles (page 24), braised in Barolo, and agnolotti (page 23). Dishes flavored with gravy, *sugo d'arrosto* (roast sauce) as it is known, are a Piedmontese specialty, which, once tried, can never been forgotten. As is bagna cauda (page 20), an intensely flavored sauce made of anchovies, butter, and garlic, into which a wide variety of fresh vegetables are dipped, and which is so spicy that it instantly awakens the palate. However, whenever the occasion merits, this region that is steeped in the ancient tradition of the former Kingdom of Savoy turns to the cuisine of the royal court to rework historical dishes, such as finanziera, a stew from the eighteenth century. But it also looks back to peasant cuisine, such as potato dumplings from the Occitan Valleys, once served plain but today superbly flavored with butter, cream, and a wonderful covering of grated Castelmagno cheese.

Bagna cauda

One of the iconic dishes of Piedmont, bagna cauda is a tasty garlic and anchovy sauce, which even boasts its own celebration day every year in Asti. Serve it with crudités for dipping.

PREPARATION TIME 30 minutes
COOKING TIME 1 hour
SERVES 4

3½ ounces/100 g salt-packed anchovy fillets
3½ fl oz/scant ½ cup/100 ml red wine
5 fl oz/scant ⅔ cup/150 ml extra-virgin olive oil
4 bulbs garlic, separated into cloves, peeled, cut in half
   lengthwise, and the germ (green shoot) removed

Soak the anchovies in a bowl of water for 5–20 minutes, then drain, remove any bones, and set aside.

Pour the red wine into a large bowl, add the anchovies, and leave to soak for a few minutes, then remove and pat dry with paper towels.

Add half the oil to a large saucepan (preferably a terracotta cooking pot), add the garlic, and stir with a wooden spoon. Add the anchovies and remaining oil and simmer for about 1 hour, stirring occasionally. Take care not to overheat the oil. Cooking should be very gentle: if possible, for better heat dispersion, use a gas burner ring under the pot. Toward the end of cooking, use a wooden spoon to break up the soft garlic cloves.

Once ready, serve in a typical *fujot* (terracotta pot), which will keep it warm.

Piedmont-style agnolotti

Small parcels of thinly rolled pasta filled with cooked meats and surrounded by a broth-style gravy, hailing from Langhe and Monferrato, are perfect for using up leftover roasted meats.

PREPARATION TIME 1 hour
COOKING TIME 2 hours 30 minutes
SERVES 6

2 tablespoons olive oil, plus 1 tablespoon peanut (groundnut) oil
1 onion, chopped
1 clove garlic, peeled and left whole
1 pound 5 ounces/600 g veal loin
14 ounces/400 g pork loin
2 × 9 oz/250 g rabbit legs
3½ fl oz/scant ½ cup/100 ml dry white wine
Sage leaves, rosemary, and 1 bay leaf tied into a bouquet garni
14 ounces/400 g spinach
10½ ounces/2½ cups/300 g grated Grana Padano cheese
10 eggs
Pinch of grated nutmeg
1 pound 12 ounces/6⅔ cups/800 g all-purpose (plain) flour

FOR THE GRAVY
1 tablespoon olive oil
1 ounce/¼ stick/30 g unsalted butter
1 pound 2 ounces/500 g veal knuckle, cut into large chunks
1 small soup/stock bone
1 onion, carrot, and celery stalk, chopped
1 clove garlic, peeled and left whole
1¾ fl oz/scant ¼ cup/50 ml red wine
1 tablespoon tomato sauce
17 fl oz/2 cups/500 ml good-quality vegetable stock, low in salt
Salt and black pepper

To make the gravy, heat the oil and butter in a large saucepan, then add the veal, bone, vegetables, and garlic, season, and cook for a few minutes. Pour in the wine, stir to deglaze the pan. Allow the wine to evaporate, then add the tomato sauce and cook slowly for about 40 minutes, gradually adding half the stock. Remove the meat pieces and discard the bone. Strain the liquid into a large bowl, and set aside.

For the filling, heat the remaining stock in a saucepan until hot. Heat the olive oil in another saucepan and add the onion and garlic. Season with salt, then add a few tablespoons of the stock and cook for 10–15 minutes.

Heat the peanut (groundnut) oil in a skillet (frying pan), add the veal, pork, and rabbit and cook until browned. Transfer to the pan with the onion, then add the wine, bouquet garni, and a little salt. Cook for 20 minutes, then moisten the meat with more stock. Do this several times, for about 50 minutes, or until the rabbit meat comes off the bone. Leave the meat to cool, then bone the rabbit and chop the meat into small pieces. Discard the bouquet garni, then add the spinach, wilt over a low heat, then chop. Add all the chopped ingredients to a bowl with two-thirds of the grated cheese and 3 eggs and combine. Season with salt and the nutmeg.

To make the pasta, gather the flour in a mound on a work surface and make a well in the center. Add 7 eggs and a pinch of salt to the well, then enough water to make a smooth dough. Mix, then knead into an elastic dough and roll out into a thin sheet. Starting from the top, place small mounds of the filling in a row on the sheet, spaced slightly apart. Fold the dough sheet over the filling and press with your fingers to seal the edges. Press on the dough between the individual mounds to seal. Using a pastry wheel, cut out the agnolotti. Cook in a saucepan of boiling salted water for 3–4 minutes, then drain. Arrange in layers in a warmed serving dish, covering each layer with gravy and the remaining grated cheese.

Taglierini with truffle

Taglierini—known as *tajarin* in Piedmontese—is a thin, noodle-like pasta with its origins in the region, first documented in the fifteenth century. Here it is served with white truffle from Alba.

PREPARATION TIME 30 minutes

COOKING TIME 15 minutes

SERVES 4

14 ounces/3⅓ cups/400 g soft wheat flour

2 eggs

3–3½ ounces/⅔–generous ¾ cup/80–100 g grated
  Grana Padano cheese

3 ounces/¾ stick/80 g butter

Pinch of grated nutmeg

A ladleful of vegetable stock

Salt and black pepper

1 Alba white truffle, shaved, to serve

Gather the flour into a mound on a clean work surface and make a well in the center. Add the eggs to the well, then sprinkle in ¼–¾ ounce/scant ⅛ cup/10–20 g of the grated cheese and pour in 3 fl oz/⅓ cup/90 ml water. Mix and knead to a fairly solid dough. Using a rolling pin, roll the dough out into a sheet and roll it up. Using a sharp knife, cut it into about ⅛-inch/3-mm wide noodles.

To make the sauce, melt the butter in a small saucepan, season it with the nutmeg, and add the remaining grated cheese. Dilute the mixture with a ladleful of stock and cook over a low heat for a few minutes, or until the sauce has the desired consistency. Season with salt and pepper and remove from the heat.

Cook the pasta in a large saucepan of boiling salted water for a few minutes until al dente, then drain, toss with the sauce, and serve topped with truffle shavings.

Buckwheat gnocchi

Gnocchi alla bava

Fresh buckwheat gnocchi smothered in a tasty fondue-style fontina cheese in a traditional Piedmontese first course. Easy to master and ideal for a dinner with friends or family lunch.

PREPARATION TIME 45 minutes
COOKING TIME 15–20 minutes
RESTING TIME 1 hour
SERVES 6

9 ounces/2 cups/250 g soft wheat flour, plus extra for dusting
9 ounces/2 cups/250 g buckwheat flour
1 egg yolk
Salt
Chopped chives, to garnish (optional)

FOR THE SAUCE
7 ounces/200 g Fontina cheese, cubed
17 fl oz/2 cups/500 ml heavy (double) cream

In a bowl, combine both flours with the egg yolk, then season with a pinch of salt and gradually add 9¼ fl oz/ generous 1 cup/270 ml water. Mix everything together with a fork, then transfer the dough to a clean work surface and continue to knead with your hands until it is a smooth and nonsticky dough. Gather it into a ball and wrap in plastic wrap (cling film). Leave to rest in the refrigerator for 1 hour.

Meanwhile, for the sauce, place the cheese and cream in a heatproof bowl set over a large saucepan of simmering water, making sure the bottom of the bowl doesn't touch the water. Stir and allow the cheese to melt over a very low heat. When the mixture takes on a light and creamy consistency, adjust the seasoning with salt only if the fondue is bland. Pour the sauce into a saucepan and heat gently.

Lightly dust a kitchen cloth with flour or lightly flour a sheet of parchment paper. Using a dough scraper, cut the dough into several portions and work each portion into a long ¾-inch/2-cm thick log. Cut each log into ¾–1¼-inch/2–3-cm long chunks and dust them with flour. Repeat until all the dough is used up. Lightly press the gnocchi, one at a time, over the tines of a floured fork with your finger to achieve the characteristic grooves. Gradually transfer the resulting gnocchi to the floured cloth or parchment paper, taking care not to overlap each other.

Bring a large saucepan of salted water to a boil, add the gnocchi, and cook for a few minutes, or until they float to the top. Remove them with a slotted spoon and put them directly into the pan with the hot sauce. Stir gently and coat well in the sauce. Serve them garnished with chopped chives, if desired.

Veal with tuna sauce

Also known as *vitel tonnato*, this is a dish of thinly sliced cold veal, which has been marinated in white wine and then boiled and topped with a creamy tuna, egg, and anchovy sauce.

PREPARATION TIME 30 minutes

COOKING TIME 1 hour 10 minutes

SERVES 6

About 2 pounds 4 ounces/1 kg veal topside
1 onion, coarsely chopped
1 carrot, coarsely chopped
1 celery stalk, coarsely chopped
½ bay leaf
Grated zest of ½ lemon and ½ orange
3½ fl oz/scant ½ cup/100 ml white wine
1¾ fl oz/scant ¼ cup/50 ml white wine vinegar
3 tablespoons extra-virgin olive oil
Cold meat stock, as needed (optional)
Salt

FOR THE SAUCE
7 ounces/200 g canned tuna in oil
4–5 oil-packed anchovy fillets
2 hard-boiled eggs, peeled
4 gherkins
Lemon juice, for blending
Extra-virgin olive oil, for blending

Place the veal in a large saucepan, add the onion, carrot, celery, bay leaf, grated zest, wine, vinegar, and oil. Just cover the contents of the pan with water or cold meat stock, place over a medium heat, and slowly bring to a boil. Cook for 30 minutes, then season with salt and cook for another 40 minutes. Remove the pan from the heat and leave the meat to cool in the liquid.

For the sauce, blend the tuna, anchovies, boiled eggs, and gherkins in a blender or food processor, adding enough lemon juice and oil to make a smooth sauce.

Drain the meat and cut it into slices. Arrange the slices in a serving dish, pour over the sauce, and serve cold. Transfer the remaining sauce to a sauce (gravy) boat and serve separately.

Rabbit with bell peppers

Rabbit is a common meat in traditional Italian dishes, and here this lean, tender meat is served in a tasty sauce of red bell peppers, bread crumbs, and red wine. Ideal to enjoy with polenta for a Sunday lunch.

PREPARATION TIME 10 minutes

COOKING TIME 1 hour 35 minutes

SERVES 4

1½ ounces/40 g stale bread
3 tablespoons extra-virgin olive oil
1 × 2 pound 4 ounce/1 kg rabbit, jointed
1 onion, chopped
1 clove garlic, peeled and left whole
2 red bell peppers, cored, seeded, and coarsely chopped
1 small sprig rosemary, chopped
1 bunch parsley, chopped
About 1¾ fl oz/scant ¼ cup/50 ml red wine
1 tablespoon superfine (caster) sugar
1 fresh red chile, finely chopped
Salt

Blitz the bread in a food processor until crumbs form, then set aside.

Heat 2 tablespoons of the oil in a large skillet (frying pan), add the rabbit, and brown on all sides for a few minutes.

Heat the remaining oil with 1 tablespoon water in another saucepan. Add the onion and garlic clove and cook for 10 minutes. Add the bell peppers and bread crumbs, then add the rosemary and some of the parsley. Cook for about 20 minutes, or until the vegetables are softened.

Meanwhile, heat the wine, sugar, chile, and a little salt in another pan until hot.

Transfer the meat to the pan with the bell peppers, add the hot wine mixture, and cook for 1 hour, adding a little extra water during cooking if needed. At the end of the cooking time, remove and discard the garlic clove. Serve the rabbit pieces with the sauce in a warmed serving dish garnished with the remaining parsley.

Mixed boiled meat

A classic Piedmontese stew consisting of a variety of slow-cooked meats. Traditional accompaniments include *bagnet ross* (Piedmontese tomato sauce), *bagnet verd* (Piedmontese herb sauce), and potatoes.

PREPARATION TIME 15 minutes

COOKING TIME 3 hours 30 minutes

SERVES 8

1 celery stalk
1 onion
1 carrot
2 pounds 4 ounces/1 kg sirloin
2 pounds 4 ounces/1 kg veal breast
½ × 3 pound 8 ounce/1.6 kg chicken
1 small veal tongue
1 small cotechino sausage
2 pounds 4 ounces/1 kg boiled calf's head
Salt

Fill a stockpot with 170 fl oz/20 cups/5 liters of salted water, add the celery, onion, and carrot and bring to a boil. Add the sirloin, reduce the heat to a simmer, and cook for 1 hour. Add the veal breast, chicken, and tongue and cook for about 2 hours over a medium heat.

Meanwhile, prick the sausage all over with a needle, then add it to another large pan of cold water, bring

to a boil, and cook for 2 hours. Turn off the heat and leave the sausage to stand in its cooking liquid for 10 minutes, then drain well.

Assemble the different meats on a large serving dish and serve with your chosen accompaniments.

Zabaglione

Every family in Italy has their own version of zabaglione, also known as zabaione—a perfectly creamy dessert that reminds many of their childhood, and one of the most popular fillings for pastries.

PREPARATION TIME 10 minutes

COOKING TIME 10 minutes

SERVES 4

3 ounces/85 g egg yolks
3 ounces/85 g superfine (caster) sugar
3 fl oz/⅓ cup/85 ml Marsala or liquor of choice

This zabaione is very quick and easy to make. Place the egg yolks and sugar in a large bowl and beat until soft, fluffy, and pale.

Add the Marsala (or liquor of your choice), transfer to a saucepan, and cook on a moderate heat until the temperature of the mixture reaches 176 °F/80 °C on a thermometer. Using a handheld mixer, whisk the mixture until it cools. Serve immediately.

Coffee bonet

Traditionally made with chocolate and crushed amaretti biscuits, this coffee version of a "bonet"— a caramel custard spoon dessert—has a beautiful balance of flavors and aromas.

PREPARATION TIME 15 minutes

COOKING TIME 1 hour 20 minutes

CHILLING TIME 3–4 hours

SERVES 6

7 fl oz/scant 1 cup/200 ml milk

14 fl oz/1⅔ cups/400 ml heavy (double) cream

3–3½ ounces/generous ⅓–scant ½ cup/80–100 g superfine (caster) sugar

8 egg yolks

2–3 tablespoons rum

5 fl oz/⅔ cup/150 ml brewed espresso

Chocolate leaves (store-bought from baking supplies stores), to decorate

FOR THE CARAMEL

3½ ounces/scant ½ cup/100 g superfine (caster) sugar

1 teaspoon lemon juice

Preheat the oven to 350 °F/180 °C/160 °C Fan/Gas 4.

For the caramel, place the sugar, 2 tablespoons of water, and the lemon juice in a small heavy-bottomed saucepan over a medium heat and allow the sugar to caramelize. Pour the caramel into a 34 fl oz/1-liter capacity loaf pan (tin) and swirl the pan to fully coat the inside.

For the custard, combine the milk, cream, and sugar in a medium saucepan and bring to a boil.

Place the egg yolks in a large heatproof bowl and mix with a ladle, then incorporate the rum, followed by the coffee. Add the milk mixture and stir to combine, then pour it into the caramel-lined pan. Place the pan inside a deep baking pan (tin) and fill the pan with enough hot water to come two-thirds of the way up the sides of the loaf pan. Bake in the preheated oven for 1 hour. Remove from the oven and set aside to cool, then chill for 3–4 hours, or ideally overnight, in the refrigerator.

Turn out, decorate with chocolate leaves, and serve.

Valle d'Aosta

Fontina cheese, the basic ingredient of all dishes

Valle d'Aosta is where the Mediterranean diet becomes distinctly Alpine. In fact, the food here is clearly influenced by climate and altitude. Pasta is almost nowhere to be found, its place taken by soups and polenta. Oil is replaced by butter and cheese. And above all, fontina is the basic ingredient of all fondues, of all fillings, of all sauces and flavorings. This cheese has a mild and fascinating taste that is heightened by the warmth of the palate. As a fondue (page 36), it is sublime as it gently adds richness with the fineness of a cream. Sweet or spicy, it is the incomparable filling of the famous Italian version of cordon bleu that is known as Valdostana (page 44). For warmth in the region's cold climate, age-old soups and stews are still made combining milk and chestnuts, turnips and rice, and onion and bread. And paying tribute to a tradition that has not been lost, there is a special dried bread that is so hard that it can only be eaten after soaking it in soup. Because of the long winters, aside from the bread, meat also had to be preserved. As a result, you can experience the flavor of the increasingly rare mocetta, a wonderful prosciutto made from chamois, goat, or ibex that pairs well with red Torrette wine, a delicious accompaniment for the whole meal. Finally, there is lardo d'Arnad, a very particular delicacy of cured pork back fat.

Valle d'Aosta-style fondue

An Italian take on the traditional Swiss fondue, made using fontina, the semi-hard cow's milk cheese famous throughout the region. Serve with a side of bread for dipping.

PREPARATION TIME 20 minutes

COOKING TIME 25 minutes

RESTING TIME 1 hour

SERVES 4

14 ounces/400 g fontina cheese, thinly sliced

7 fl oz/scant 1 cup/200 ml milk, plus more as needed

1½ ounces/3 tablespoons/40 g cold unsalted butter, cut into small pieces

4 egg yolks

White truffle, for shaving (optional)

Salt and white pepper

Slices of pane nero (dark rye bread), toasted, to serve

Put the cheese into a large bowl. Add the milk (more may be required as the liquid must cover the cheese), cover, and leave to stand for 1 hour.

Without draining too much, transfer the cheese to a heat-proof bowl and add the cold butter. Place the bowl over a pan of simmering water, making sure the bottom doesn't touch the water, allowing the cheese to melt while stirring constantly. A compact mass will form at first before slowly turning liquid as it melts. When the mixture has reached a creamy consistency, briskly stir in one egg yolk at a time, then leave it over the simmering water for 2–3 minutes so that the mixture acquires its typical velvety appearance (at this point, you can decide whether to add a little of the soaking milk if the consistency is too thick). Adjust the seasoning with salt and just a pinch of pepper if you plan to add truffle afterward; otherwise, add more pepper.

Divide the fondue between warmed bowls and scatter truffle shavings over the top, if desired. Serve with toasted slices of dark rye bread, which should be wrapped in a napkin to keep them warm.

Savoy cabbage soup

Zuppa di cavolo verza

An ideal first course when the weather starts to turn cold, this soup is typical of the Aosta Valley region, made with layers of Savoy cabbage, the local fontina cheese, and leftover bread.

PREPARATION TIME 20 minutes

COOKING TIME 40 minutes

RESTING TIME 10 minutes

SERVES 4

8 thick slices whole wheat (wholemeal) bread

2 cloves garlic, peeled and left whole

Unsalted butter, for greasing, spreading, and topping

2 tablespoons extra-virgin olive oil

1 Savoy cabbage, about 1 pound 5 ounces/1 pound 9 ounces/600–700 g, cut into strips

34 fl oz/4¼ cups/1 liter vegetable stock

7 ounces/200 g smoked pancetta, chopped

7 ounces/200 g fontina cheese, sliced

Grated Grana Padano cheese, for sprinkling

Salt and black pepper

Preheat the broiler (grill) to medium heat. Rub the bread slices with a garlic clove, then spread them with butter and toast them lightly under the broiler. Remove and set aside.

Preheat the oven to 350 °F/180 °C/160 °C Fan/Gas 4. Grease a large ovenproof dish with butter.

Heat the oil in a large saucepan, add the remaining garlic clove, and cook for a few minutes until browned, then remove the garlic and discard. Add the cabbage to the pan, season with salt and a little pepper, and sauté for 2–3 minutes. Pour in the stock, then bring to a boil and cook the cabbage for 5–6 minutes until tender. Drain well, setting the stock aside in a bowl or jug.

Add the pancetta to a nonstick skillet (frying pan) and brown until it turns translucent. Drain off the excess fat.

Arrange four slices of toasted bread over the bottom of the prepared dish. Layer half the pancetta, cooked cabbage, and sliced cheese over the bread, then cover with the remaining slices of bread. Layer the remaining pancetta, cabbage, and sliced cheese over the bread and drizzle with the reserved stock. Finish with grated Grana Padano cheese and a few curls of butter.

Bake in the preheated oven for 10 minutes, then turn on the broiler again and broil for 20 minutes, or until the top is golden brown. Remove from the oven and set it aside to rest for at least 10 minutes. Serve in the same dish at the table.

Cheese polenta

A tasty, hearty traditional dish of polenta and cheese that is perfect for recharging the batteries on cold winter days. The secret to the perfect dish is to keep stirring to achieve a soft, smooth consistency.

PREPARATION TIME 10 minutes

COOKING TIME 55 minutes

SERVES 4–6

9 ounces/2 cups/250 g coarse cornmeal (polenta)
5½ ounces/150 g Toma cheese, cubed
7 ounces/200 g fontina cheese, cubed
3½ ounces/100 g unsalted butter
Coarse salt

For the cornmeal (polenta), bring a large saucepan of salted water to a boil according to the package directions (on average, 4 parts water is required for 1 part cornmeal, so about 34 fl oz/4¼ cups/1 liter water here). While stirring the water briskly with a whisk, sprinkle in the cornmeal. Watch closely to prevent the formation of lumps. As soon as the cornmeal has absorbed the water evenly, use a wooden spoon to continue to stir for 45 minutes, or until the cornmeal is cooked. It should look creamy and the grains will be tender when done.

Once the polenta is cooked, add the cheese cubes and stir to incorporate.

Melt the butter in a skillet (frying pan) over a low heat until it turns golden brown.

Divide the polenta between bowls, add the browned butter as desired, and serve.

Ratatouille

Based on the Provençal dish of stewed mixed vegetables, and born of peasant traditions, this Valle d'Aosta version oven bakes the carrots, potatoes, and green beans found in the region.

PREPARATION TIME 30 minutes
COOKING TIME 1 hour 20 minutes
SERVES 4

Unsalted butter, for greasing and topping
12 ounces/350 g potatoes, preferably Ollomont, peeled and cut
    into slices ⅛ inch/3–4 mm thick
12 ounces/350 g carrots, peeled and cut into slices
    ⅛ inch/3–4 mm thick
12 ounces/350 g green beans, trimmed
A few fresh sage leaves, chopped, for sprinkling
1–2 dried bay leaves, crumbled, for sprinkling (optional)
Salt and black pepper

Preheat the oven to 350 °F/180 °C/160 °C Fan/Gas 4.

Grease an ovenproof dish well with butter and arrange the vegetables inside as shown opposite. Sprinkle over a few chopped sage leaves (and a little dried and crumbled bay leaves if you like, but add them sparingly because the flavor is strong), top with curls of butter, and season with salt and pepper.

Bake in the preheated oven for 1 hour 20 minutes, or until the vegetables are tender. Serve at the table.

Marinated trout

Trote in carpione

"*Carpione*" refers to a pickling or preserving process traditional to Valle d'Aosta, and here trout fillets are floured and fried, then marinated for 24 hours in white wine and vinegar

PREPARATION TIME 30 minutes

COOKING TIME 25 minutes

RESTING TIME 24 hours

SERVES 4

All-purpose (plain) flour, for coating
4 trout, filleted and heads removed
4 tablespoons olive oil, plus extra for frying the fish
1 clove garlic, peeled and left whole
2 onions, chopped or thinly sliced
A few fresh sage leaves
17 fl oz/2 cups/500 ml dry white wine
17 fl oz/2 cups/500 ml white wine vinegar
Salt

Spread enough flour out on a large plate for coating the fish, then toss the fish in the flour until lightly coated. Heat enough oil for frying the fish in a large, deep saucepan until hot. Carefully add the fish and fry for a few minutes, then remove with a slotted spoon or skimmer and drain on paper towels.

Heat the 4 tablespoons oil in a large pan, add the garlic clove, and cook for a few minutes until browned, then remove and discard the garlic. Add the onions and sage leaves, followed by the trout. Season with salt and cook over a low heat for about 10 minutes, until ready. Remove the fish from the pan and set aside to cool. Set the cooking liquid and onions aside.

Arrange the cooled trout, cooking liquid, and onions in alternating layers in a large terrine. Mix the wine and vinegar together well in a jug, then pour the mixture into the terrine. Cover and leave to marinate in the refrigerator overnight. Serve in the terrine.

Venison stew

Braised venison Valle d'Aosta-style is marinated
in the refrigerator for two days, then cooked in
a rich sauce of red wine, tomatoes, and cream,
flavored with grappa.

PREPARATION TIME 30 minutes
COOKING TIME 1 hour 20 minutes
RESTING TIME 48 hours
SERVES 8

3 pounds 5 ounces/1.5 kg boned leg or shoulder of venison,
   cut into small cubes
2 cloves garlic, finely chopped
1 onion, thinly sliced into rings
1 carrot, cut into small pieces
1 celery stalk, cut into small pieces
1 sprig parsley, finely chopped
1 dried bay leaf, crumbled
1 sprig thyme
2 cloves
2 juniper berries
5 black peppercorns
1 bottle (25 fl oz/750 ml) red wine
4 tablespoons vegetable oil
2¾ fl oz/80 ml or 2 shot glasses grappa
All-purpose (plain) flour, for sprinkling
1 pound 2 ounces/500 g skinned tomatoes
8 fl oz/1 cup/250 ml heavy (double) cream
Salt and black pepper

Place the venison in a large bowl. Add the garlic,
onion, carrot, celery, parsley, bay leaf, thyme sprig,
cloves, juniper berries, peppercorns, and a pinch of salt.
Pour in the wine, cover with plastic wrap (cling film),
and leave to marinate in the refrigerator for 2 days,
stirring occasionally.

Remove the meat from the marinade and leave to drain.
Strain the remaining marinade through a fine-mesh
strainer (sieve) into a bowl or jug and set aside.

Heat the oil in a large saucepan, add the meat, and
brown on all sides. Drizzle with the grappa and allow
it to evaporate. Sprinkle the meat with a little flour and
add the strained marinade. Add the tomatoes, season
with salt and pepper, and cook for about 1 hour.

Transfer the cooked meat to a serving dish. Add the
cream to the cooking liquid and allow the resulting
sauce to heat up and thicken, then pour the sauce over
the meat. Serve.

Cheese-stuffed veal cutlets

A specialty of Valle d'Aosta—the region's famous fontina cheese is sandwiched in a butterflied and breaded veal cutlet, then pan-fried in this hearty Alpine version of the cordon bleu dish.

PREPARATION TIME 15 minutes

COOKING TIME 20 minutes

SERVES 4

4 thick slices fontina cheese

4 veal cutlets (chops); ask your butcher to cut four thick bone-in
   rib chops and to butterfly them, leaving them joined at the bone

All-purpose (plain) flour, for coating

2 eggs, beaten

Bread crumbs, for coating

3½ ounces/100 g unsalted butter, for cooking

Salt and black pepper

Lemon wedges, to serve

Lay a slice of cheese on one half of each veal cutlet (chop), cover with the other half, and press the edges of the meat well to prevent the cheese from escaping when cooked.

Season the cutlets with salt and pepper on both sides. Spread the flour out on a large plate, add the beaten eggs to a shallow bowl and season lightly, and spread the bread crumbs out on another plate. Gently toss each cutlet in the flour to lightly coat, then dip them into the eggs and toss in the bread crumbs until coated all over.

Melt the butter in a large skillet (frying pan) over a low heat until frothy. Add the cutlets and brown them gently on both sides until cooked through and the cheese is melted, about 20 minutes. Remove from the pan and drain on paper towels, then arrange in a serving dish with lemon wedges and serve piping hot.

Mont Blanc

When chestnut season arrives in Valle d'Aosta during the fall (autumn), this famous dessert of chestnut purée topped with a mountain of whipped cream—named for the highest snowy Alpine peak—is served.

PREPARATION TIME 30 minutes

COOKING TIME 20 minutes

SERVES 10

3 pounds/generous 11 cups/1.5 kg chestnuts, washed
1¼ ounces/⅓ cup/35 g unsweetened cocoa powder
2¼ ounces/¼ cup/60 g superfine (caster) sugar
1 tablespoon rum
Whipped cream, for topping
Meringues and/or marrons glacés, for topping

Score the skin of the chestnuts with a knife. Boil them in a large saucepan of water for 20 minutes, or until they are cooked through but still firm. Drain the chestnuts and peel them, taking care to also remove the inner skin (soaking them for a few seconds in a bowl of ice water makes this task easier).

Mash the peeled chestnuts to a paste in a food mill, then mix with the cocoa powder, sugar, and rum. Pass the mixture through the food mill a second time.

Divide the mixture among small glasses for individual servings or arrange it in the shape of a mountain in a larger serving dish. Top with whipped cream, meringues, and/or marrons glacés as desired.

Liguria

The scent of basil from east to west

All along the enchanting arc formed by the Ligurian coastline, from the Riviera di Levante in the east to the Riviera di Ponente in the west, there is a scent of basil, the herb that is crushed in a mortar with oil, garlic, and pine nuts—and almost always Parmesan cheese—to make pesto (page 50), the incredible sauce that makes every pasta a delicacy and every minestrone a special treat. This sauce is enjoyed and copied the world over. Liguria has so much sea and so little land—the former offers a bounty of fish, both of little and great value, to be eaten fresh or salted and preserved, while the latter is miserly, its stony soil only subdued by tilling in narrow strips that descend in terraces to the shore. Here, humans have performed the miracle of cultivating olive trees and vineyards whose fruit ripen to create the truly exquisite flavors found in the region's particularly light and fragrant oil, and in the extraordinary amber-tinged wines, such as the outstanding Passito wine Sciacchetrà, made in the Cinque Terre from dried grapes, with the aroma of apricots and cocoa. While the region is known for the simplicity of its cuisine, its dishes are only simple in appearance. Highlights include focaccia, particularly the variety from Recco (page 53); farinata, tasty chickpea flour pancakes typical of Savona (page 54); and fresh pasta, such as trofie from Genoa.

Trofie with pesto

Trofie is an iconic pasta shape, believed to have originated in the vicinity of Golfo Paradiso, and traditionally served with pesto in this quintessential Ligurian starter full of flavor and color.

PREPARATION TIME 40 minutes

COOKING TIME 6–15 minutes

RESTING TIME 30 minutes

SERVES 4–6

1 pound 2 ounces/generous 4 cups/500 g Italian "00" flour

FOR THE PESTO

1 clove garlic, chopped

3 tablespoons pine nuts

4 fl oz/½ cup/120 ml extra-virgin olive oil, plus extra for drizzling

scant 3 cups/2½ ounces/70 g basil leaves, plus extra to serve

½ cup/2 ounces/60 g grated Parmesan or pecorino cheese

Salt

For the pesto, pulse the garlic, pine nuts, and a little of the oil in a blender or food processor a few times, scraping down the sides of the bowl. Add the basil and a little more oil and pulse a few times, then add the cheese. While the machine is still running, slowly add the remaining olive oil in a thin, steady stream until it is all incorporated and smooth. Season with salt and transfer to a small, clean jar. Drizzle a little olive oil on the top and chill in the refrigerator. It should last for up to a week in the refrigerator.

Place the flour in a large bowl, make a well in the center, and gradually add 7 fl oz/scant 1 cup /200 ml lukewarm water while stirring with a fork. Knead the dough by hand until it is smooth and compact. Cover with plastic wrap (cling film) and leave to rest at room temperature for at least 30 minutes.

Take a small portion of the dough and hold it in your fist to keep it moist and warm, then remove a much smaller piece from it. Place this piece on a pastry board and roll it on the board under your palm and fingers until it has an elongated shape. Tilt your hand slightly to give the piece its typical twist, or "curl," and repeat the process until all the dough is used up.

You can either dry the pasta (in which case it will need 15 minutes to cook), or cook it fresh in a large saucepan of boiling salted water for 6–10 minutes, depending on its thickness, until al dente. Drain the pasta, transfer to a large bowl, and mix with plenty of pesto. You can also drizzle the pasta with additional oil to help coat the pasta with pesto. Serve topped with extra basil leaves.

Recco-style focaccia

Focaccia di Recco—a type of flatbread filled with crescenza cheese—is a delicacy whose popularity extends far beyond the borders of Liguria. The recipe takes patience and dexterity, but is worth the effort.

PREPARATION TIME 30 minutes

COOKING TIME 15 minutes

RESTING TIME 1 hour 5 minutes

SERVES 6

14 ounces/400 g Manitoba flour (strong white bread flour), plus extra for dusting

4 fl oz/½ cup/120 ml extra-virgin olive oil

14 ounces/400 g very fresh Ligurian crescenza (stracchino) cheese, cut into small pieces

Salt

To make the focaccia, add the flour and 2¾ fl oz/⅓ cup/ 80 ml of the olive oil to a large bowl and mix together, then add 7 fl oz/scant 1 cup/200 ml water until you can work it into a soft dough. Cover with a kitchen cloth and leave to rest for 1 hour away from drafts. Knead again, gather the dough into a ball, cover again, and leave it to rest for another 5 minutes.

Divide the dough in two and roll out each piece into a very thin sheet on a very lightly floured work surface. The rule is that the dough sheets are stretched by pulling them with closed hands underneath, and the pulling motion creates a translucent dough. Start by using a rolling pin, but continue with your hands to avoid using too much flour and to get super-thin sheets.

To cook the focaccia, you will need a *testo*, which is a round tin-plated copper tray on which to place one of the dough sheets after it has been properly oiled.

Using your hands, dot small pieces of cheese over the dough, then cover the filling with the second dough sheet.

Preheat the oven to its highest temperature setting.

The top sheet must be pinched to create perforations that serve as steam vents. After spreading the rest of the oil evenly over the surface, use your palm to press lightly on the cheese so that it spreads well. Sprinkle the focaccia evenly with salt and bake in the preheated oven for 15 minutes, or until golden brown and its texture is crispy and crumbly. Serve immediately.

Farinata

Farinata, or *fainà* as they say in Genoa, is an iconic street food found in the Ligurian capital. A savory pancake made using chickpea flour, it is delicious fresh out of the oven, making it an ideal snack on the go.

PREPARATION TIME 20 minutes
COOKING TIME 22–27 minutes
RESTING TIME 4–6 hours
SERVES 6

7 ounces/1½ cups/190 g chickpea flour
1¾ fl oz/scant ¼ cup/50 ml extra-virgin olive oil, plus extra
  for greasing
¼ ounce/2 teaspoons/10 g salt
2 sprigs rosemary, leaves picked (optional)

Place the chickpea flour in a large bowl, pour in 17 fl oz/ 2 cups/500 ml water, and mix together with a whisk. The batter should be runny but lump-free. A foam will form on the surface, which should be removed with a skimmer or slotted spoon, but take care to only remove the foam, so as not to reduce the amount of batter. Leave the batter to rest at room temperature for 4–6 hours, stirring every hour with a whisk and always skimming off the foam on the surface. These steps are very important to keep the batter smooth and prevent the water and flour from separating.

After resting, add the oil, salt, and rosemary, if using, and mix well until combined.

Preheat the oven to 480 °F/250 °C/230 °C Fan/Gas 10. Grease a 12½-inch/32-cm light aluminum baking pan (tin) with oil.

Pour the batter into the prepared pan and bake in the preheated oven on the lowest oven shelf for 12 minutes. Reduce the oven temperature to 400 °F/200 °C/180 °C Fan/Gas 6, move the pan to the second oven shelf, and bake for another 10–15 minutes until the classic amber crust forms on the surface. Remove the farinata from the oven and leave to cool before cutting it into slices and serving.

Cuttlefish in tomato sauce

Seppie in zimino

An easy and delicious dish of cuttlefish, Swiss chard, and tomato. "*In zimino*," believed to be derived from the Arabic "*samin,*" meaning "thick sauce," refers to the method of cooking, and there are many variants.

PREPARATION TIME 20 minutes

COOKING TIME 45 minutes

SERVES 4

4 tablespoons extra-virgin olive oil
½ celery stalk, finely chopped
¼ onion, finely chopped
1 small sprig parsley, finely chopped
3 bunches Swiss chard, stems removed and leaves cut into
  small pieces
1 pound 5 ounces/600 g cuttlefish, cleaned, gutted, washed, dried
  with paper towels, and cut into strips
9 ounces/250 g plum tomatoes, puréed and strained
Salt and black pepper

Heat the oil in a large skillet (frying pan) with a lid, add the celery, onion, and parsley, and sauté for 5 minutes. Add the chard, stir, and cook for about 10 minutes. Add the cuttlefish and tomatoes. Season with salt and pepper and mix together. Bring to a boil, then reduce the heat to low, cover, and cook for about 30 minutes until tender and flavorful.

Remove the pan from the heat, transfer the contents to a serving dish, and serve immediately.

Stuffed veal breast

Cima ripiena

A famous Genoese dish, originally designed to use up leftovers, of veal breast stuffed with meats, cheese, and vegetables. Served in slices, this is a striking-looking dish.

PREPARATION TIME 45 minutes

COOKING TIME 2 hours 20 minutes

SERVES 6

About 2 pounds/900 g veal breast, with a slit cut into the center to create a pocket
1 onion
1 carrot
2 dried bay leaves

FOR THE STUFFING
7 ounces/200 g Swiss chard
7 ounces/200 g veal sweetbreads
3½ ounces/2 cups/100 g bread crumbs
Milk, for soaking
2 ounces/50 g lardo (cured pork back fat), chopped
2 eggs
1½ ounces/⅓ cup/40 g grated Grana Padano cheese
7 ounces/generous ¾ cup/200 g ground (minced) veal
2 tablespoons pine nuts
3 tablespoons shelled fresh peas
2 tablespoons chopped marjoram
Salt and black pepper

For the stuffing, cook the Swiss chard in a large saucepan of boiling salted water for 2 minutes, then drain, squeeze out the water, and chop it up. Set aside. Cook the sweetbreads in another large saucepan of lightly salted water for a few minutes, then drain and dice. Soak the bread crumbs in a bowl of milk until soft, then squeeze to drain.

Place the Swiss chard, sweetbreads, bread crumbs, and back fat together in a large bowl, then add the eggs, cheese, ground (minced) veal, pine nuts, peas, and marjoram. Season with salt and pepper and gently mix until combined. Fill the veal pocket with the stuffing, sew the pocket opening closed with kitchen twine (string), and tie up the meat like a roast.

Fill a large saucepan with 101 fl oz/12 cups/3 liters cold water, add the onion, carrot, and bay leaves, then add the veal, and simmer for a good 2 hours.

Drain the meat, place it between two plates, with a weight on top to give it the typical flattened shape, and set it aside to cool.

Cut the stuffed pocket into slices, about ½ inch/1 cm thick, arrange them on a serving dish, and serve.

Rabbit with olives

Coniglio alle olive

A very tasty meat main course dish that involves cooking the rabbit in a rich sauce of Taggiasche olives and herbs, enhanced by the texture and subtle flavor of chopped liver. Perfect to share with the whole family.

PREPARATION TIME 30 minutes

COOKING TIME 45 minutes

SERVES 4

1 rabbit with its liver, about 2 pounds 4 ounces/1 kg
3½ fl oz/scant ½ cup/100 ml extra-virgin olive oil
1 small sprig rosemary, chopped
2 cloves garlic, peeled and left whole
1 bay leaf
7 fl oz/scant 1 cup/200 ml red wine
2 tomatoes, skinned, halved, seeded, and cut into small dice
3½ ounces/generous ¾ cup/100 g Taggiasche olives
Vegetable stock, for moistening
Salt and black pepper

Start by cutting the meat into pieces, setting aside the liver (this can also be done by the butcher). Wash the pieces and dry them thoroughly with paper towels. Chop the liver with a knife and set it aside. Rub the pieces of meat with salt and pepper. Pour the oil into a large saucepan with a lid, add the rosemary, garlic, and bay leaf, and place the pan over a medium heat. Add the pieces of meat and cook, turning them so that they brown evenly. When the meat has turned a golden color, pour in the wine, and allow it to evaporate. Cover the pan with a lid and cook for 20 minutes.

Add the chopped liver, tomatoes, and olives to the pan, partially cover with the lid, and cook over a medium heat for another 20–25 minutes, moistening the meat occasionally with a little hot stock. When cooked, turn off the heat, rest for a few minutes, then serve.

Cherry jam tart

A classic and stunning Ligurian dessert of cherry jam sandwiched between two layers of sweet shortcut pastry with shapes of your choice cut from the top layer to reveal the deep red color of the jam beneath.

PREPARATION TIME 45 minutes

COOKING TIME 25 minutes

SERVES 6

10½ ounces/2¾ sticks/300 g butter, softened and cut into pieces, plus extra for greasing

1 pound/3¾ cups/450 g all-purpose (plain) flour, plus extra for dusting

6 ounces/generous ¾ cup/180 g granulated sugar

Grated zest of ½ lemon

9 ounces/scant 1 cup/250 g cherry jam

Confectioners' (icing) sugar, for dusting

Preheat the oven to 400 °F/200 °C/180 °C Fan/Gas 4. Grease two large baking sheets with butter and dust with flour.

On a clean work surface or in a bowl, add the flour and granulated sugar, a little grated lemon zest, and the butter, and quickly mix, then knead to form a dough. Divide the dough in half.

Roll out one-half of the pastry into a disk, and place it on one of the prepared baking sheets. Cut out star or flower shapes (or other designs), gently removing the cutouts (offcuts) and adding them to the second half of the dough. Roll this second disk to the same size as the first, and place it on the other baking sheet. Bake both disks in the preheated oven for 25 minutes, or until the pastry is a slight golden color. Remove and leave to cool.

Spread the jam on the surface of the whole pastry disk without cutouts, then cover it with the other disk and press so that the "holes" are filled with jam. Sprinkle the top with plenty of confectioners' (icing) sugar, then transfer the cake to a serving plate and serve.

Lombardy

Much more than yellow risotto and red bresaola

Lombardy is a rich land, where rice is king in the Pavia and Lomellina areas, and polenta abounds in the Seriana Valley. It is a land where milk flows in rivers, thickening into excellent cheeses with precise and distinctive flavors, such as the "teary" Grana Lodigiano, with drops of whey emerging like mother-of-pearl immediately after cutting; Taleggio, whose marriage with pears must be happily consummated; as well as age-old bitto and soft mascarpone. And, without exaggeration, thin slices of bresaola, the acknowledged queen of the Valtellina region, are like red rose petals.

The flavors of the land have been assimilated by the region's cities and turned into tasty dishes. As a result, we have the unmissable yellow risotto from Milan (page 64); the ancient polenta taragna (page 66), which in Brescia goes from peasant dish to high-class thanks to the addition of puina (a product of the ricotta cheese making process) and bagoss (a cheese produced only in Bagolino); the unusual pumpkin tortelli of Mantua (page 67), with its intriguing bittersweet flavor; and pizzoccheri (page 68) from Valtellina, a type of short tagliatelle made with a blend of buckwheat flour and wheat flour and plenty of cheese. Then there are the wines from Oltrepò Pavese and Valtellina, and others made from the prized vineyards of Franciacorta, in the province of Brescia, which over time has also become a land of much-enjoyed and exquisite sparkling wines.

Saffron risotto

This bright yellow risotto is one of the most emblematic first course dishes of the Lombardy region. It is similar to a traditional saffron risotto, but distinguished by the addition of bone marrow.

PREPARATION TIME 10 minutes
COOKING TIME 25 minutes
STEEPING TIME 1 hour
SERVES 4

1 sachet saffron threads
50 fl oz/6¼ cups/1.5 liters lukewarm meat stock
¾ ounce/20 g veal bone marrow
2¼ ounces/½ stick/60 g unsalted butter
1 small onion, finely chopped
11 ounces/1¾ cups/320 g Carnaroli rice
2¼ ounces/½ cup/60 g grated Grana Padano or Parmesan cheese

In a bowl or cup, place the saffron threads in 8 fl oz/ 1 cup/250 ml of the lukewarm meat stock and leave to steep for at least 1 hour. This will allow them to release their intense yellow color. Meanwhile, use a knife to extract the marrow from the bones and cut it into chunks.

Melt 1 ounce/¼ stick/30 g of the butter with the bone marrow in a large saucepan with a lid. Add the onion and sauté over a very low heat until the onion turns translucent. Add the rice and stir so that it absorbs the butter and onion and becomes glossy. Add a ladleful of the lukewarm stock and half-cook the rice, adding another ladleful of stock when the previous one has been absorbed. Next, add the saffron together with 1–2 tablespoons of the stock, then finish cooking the rice, adding a ladleful of stock at a time until it is all used up.

When the rice is cooked (this should take 15–18 minutes), remove the pan from the heat and stir in the remaining butter until the risotto has a creamy consistency. Add the grated cheese, then cover and leave the risotto to rest for a few minutes. Transfer the risotto to a warmed serving dish and serve immediately.

Taragna-style polenta

A popular dish typical of the Upper Lombardy region, especially the valleys of the province of Bergamo and the Valtellina Valley, it differs from the classic polenta in its use of buckwheat flour, milk, butter, and cheese.

PREPARATION TIME 20 minutes

COOKING TIME 45 minutes–1 hour

SERVES 4

3½ fl oz/scant ½ cup/100 ml milk
2 ounces/scant ½ cup/50 g coarsely ground cornmeal (polenta)
3½ ounces/generous ¾ cup/100 g buckwheat flour
1 ounce/2 tablespoons/30 g unsalted butter
A few sage leaves
3 ounces/80 g Formai de Mut or Branzi cheese, cut into cubes
Salt

Combine 14 fl oz/1¾ cups/400 ml water, the milk, and a little salt in a large saucepan or copper pot and bring to a boil. Sprinkle in the cornmeal (polenta) and buckwheat flour and cook for 40–45 minutes while mixing with a whisk.

Place the butter in a small saucepan with the sage and heat gently until the butter has melted. Remove the sage with a slotted spoon and discard, then add the melted butter to the polenta mixture. Add the cheese and stir in until it is completely melted; the result should be stringy. Serve immediately.

Pumpkin tortelli

Ideal for a special occasion, this filled egg pasta dish is a speciality from Mantua. The unmistakable flavor comes from the use of Mantuan fruit mustard and amaretti biscuits in the filling.

PREPARATION TIME 1 hour
COOKING TIME 1 hour
RESTING TIME 30 minutes
SERVES 4

FOR THE PASTA DOUGH
7 ounces/1⅓ cups/200 g all-purpose (plain) flour, plus extra
  for dusting
2 eggs
1 egg yolk

FOR THE FILLING
1 pound 5 ounces/600 g yellow pumpkin, such as Delica, skinned,
  seeded, and cut into large chunks
7 ounces/200 g strong Mantuan fruit mustard, finely chopped

1 egg yolk
7 ounces/200 g amaretti biscuits, crushed to a fine powder
3½ ounces/1¼ cups/100 g grated Parmesan cheese
Grated nutmeg
Salt and black pepper

TO FINISH
2¼ ounces/½ stick/60 g butter
Grated Parmesan cheese, plus extra to serve

For the pasta dough, gather the flour into a mound on a clean work surface and make a well in the center. Add the eggs and egg yolk to the well and mix and knead to a smooth and elastic dough. Cover the dough in plastic wrap (cling film) and set it aside to rest at room temperature for at least 30 minutes.

Preheat the oven to 425 °F/220 °C/200 °C Fan/Gas 7. Line a large baking sheet with parchment paper.

For the filling, spread the pumpkin chunks out on the prepared baking sheet and bake in the preheated oven for 30–40 minutes until tender. Remove from the oven and set aside to cool. It is very important to dry the pumpkin out well.

Place the cooled pumpkin into a large bowl and mash well to the consistency of a purée. Add the fruit mustard, egg yolk, amaretti biscuits, grated cheese, and plenty of nutmeg. Adjust the seasoning with salt and pepper and mix everything well until combined.

Dust a large baking sheet with flour. Using a rolling pin or pasta machine, roll the dough out into a thin sheet, then using a pastry wheel, cut out a few pasta strips, about 2½ inches/6 cm wide, at a time. Place hazelnut-size balls of stuffing spaced 1½–2 inches/4–5 cm apart on top of one strip, then cover with a second strip and press down with your fingertips to seal the edges well while allowing all the air to escape. Use the pastry wheel to cut out the individual tortelli and lay them out on the prepared baking sheet.

To finish, place the butter in a large saucepan and melt over a low heat. Meanwhile, bring a large saucepan of salted water to a boil, add the tortelli, and cook for a few minutes. Drain with a slotted spoon and transfer to the saucepan with the melted butter. Add a handful of grated cheese and toss the tortelli until they are coated all over.

Arrange the tortelli on serving plates and finish with a sprinkling of black pepper and extra grated Parmesan.

Pizzoccheri with cheese

A classic dish of the Valtellina Valley in the Lombardy region, pizzoccheri is a fettucine-style pasta made from buckwheat and wheat flours, served with potato, cabbage, and cheese.

PREPARATION TIME 30 minutes

COOKING TIME 45 minutes

SERVES 4

4 ounces/1 cup/120 g buckwheat flour
2 ounces/scant ½ cup/50 g soft wheat flour
2 eggs
Milk
1 large potato, sliced
¼ cabbage, cut into strips
9 ounces/250 g Swiss chard or spinach, chopped
3 ounces/¾ stick/80 g unsalted butter
4–5 sage leaves
1 clove garlic, peeled and left whole
5 ounces/150 g Bitto or Casera cheese, thinly sliced
Salt
Grated Grana Padano cheese, to serve

For the pasta dough, gather the flours into a mound on a clean work surface and make a well in the center. Add the eggs and enough milk to make a soft dough, and mix, then knead until a dough forms. Roll the dough out into a sheet that is not too thin, then fold the sheet several times and slice it into ribbons similar to wide fettuccine.

Boil the potato, cabbage, and chard in a large saucepan of lightly salted water for 30 minutes.

Add the freshly made pizzoccheri, which needs only a few minutes to cook, calculating that the vegetables and pasta should be done at the same time. Drain everything well.

To serve the pasta, melt the butter in a medium skillet (frying pan), add the sage leaves and garlic, and sauté until the garlic turns golden. Remove and discard the garlic.

In a warmed soup tureen, make a layer of pizzoccheri with the vegetables, drizzle with a little of the melted butter, and spread the thinly sliced cheese on top. Repeat the layers until all the ingredients are used up. Serve with a generous helping of grated cheese.

Beet and potato salad

A quick, easy-to-prepare dish of cooked beets (beetroot) and potatoes dressed with oil and vinegar, ideal for a simple, nutritious lunch or for serving alongside fish dishes.

PREPARATION TIME 10 minutes
COOKING TIME 20–25 minutes
SERVES 4–6

2 medium potatoes, unpeeled
2 cooked beets (beetroot), peeled
Extra-virgin olive oil
White wine vinegar
Salt and black pepper

Cook the potatoes in a large saucepan of boiling water for 20–25 minutes until tender but still firm. Drain and leave to cool completely before peeling them. Cut the potatoes and beets (beetroot) into thin slices of the same thickness if possible.

Arrange the potatoes and beets in a serving dish, alternating the slices for visual appeal. Dress with oil and vinegar, then season with salt and a sprinkling of pepper and serve.

Perch with sage

Milan is the regional capital of Lombardy, and this simple dish of fried perch, a fish found in all the major lakes of the region, is a specialty of the city, served with a beautiful sage butter.

PREPARATION TIME 20 minutes
COOKING TIME 15 minutes
MARINATING TIME 1 hour
SERVES 6

12 perch fillets
3 fl oz/scant ½ cup/95 ml olive oil
Juice of 1 lemon
1 scallion (spring onion), finely chopped
All-purpose (plain) flour, for coating
2 eggs, beaten
Bread crumbs, for coating
1 ounce/¼ stick/30 g unsalted butter
A handful of fresh sage leaves
Salt and black pepper

Arrange the fish fillets in a single layer on a large plate. In a bowl, whisk 1¾ fl oz/scant ¼ cup/50 ml of the oil with the lemon juice and the scallion (spring onion) to form an emulsion, then pour it over the fillets. Cover with plastic wrap (cling film) and leave to marinate in the refrigerator for 1 hour.

Drain and dry the fillets with paper towels. Spread the flour out on a large plate, add the beaten eggs to a shallow bowl and lightly season with salt, and spread the bread crumbs out on another large plate. Toss each fish fillet first into the flour, then dip into the eggs, and finally toss in the bread crumbs until coated all over.

Heat half the butter and the remaining oil in a large skillet (frying pan). Add the fish in batches and fry on both sides until golden. Drain and arrange them in a warmed serving dish.

Melt the remaining butter in the skillet, add the sage leaves, and leave to steep for a few minutes, then pour the sauce over the fish. Serve immediately.

Almond crumb cake

The word *sbrisolona* comes from the Italian *sbriciolaire*, meaning "to crumble." Typically associated with the city of Mantua, variations of this dish can be found throughout the region.

PREPARATION TIME 20 minutes
COOKING TIME 40 minutes
SERVES 6

7 ounces/1¾ sticks/200 g unsalted butter, cut into small pieces, plus extra for greasing
7 ounces/1⅔ cups/200 g soft wheat flour
7 ounces/1⅔ cups/200 g fine maize flour
6 ounces/generous ¾ cup/180 g superfine (caster) sugar
7 ounces/1½ cups/200 g unblanched almonds, coarsely chopped
2 egg yolks
Grated zest of 1 lemon
Salt

Preheat the oven to 350 °F/180 °C/160 °C Fan/Gas 4. Grease a 10½-inch/26-cm springform cake pan (tin) with butter.

Add both flours, the sugar, and a pinch of salt to a large bowl and mix together until combined. Mix in the chopped almonds.

Make a well in the center of the mixture and add the egg yolks. Add the grated lemon zest together with the butter and mix everything together with your hands, then knead to form a dough consisting of large crumbs.

Fill the prepared cake pan with the crumble dough, gently levelling it out without compacting it, and bake in the preheated oven for about 40 minutes. Remove and leave the cake to cool completely still in its pan.

Transfer to a serving plate and use your hands to break it up into portions.

Trentino-Alto Adige

A whirlwind of speck, dumplings, and polenta

Trentino-Alto Adige, from Val Venosta to Rovereto, is a marvelous expanse of Reinette du Canada, Golden Delicious, and Stark Delicious apples. Here apples are not just fruit but also appetizers (starters) and side dishes, sauces and jams and drinks, as well as the incomparable filling for strudels. But as you begin to climb and the mountain air awakens the senses, the pervading scent becomes that of elegant smoked speck, followed by a whirlwind of sweet and savory dumplings and polenta in a hundred different ways. Wine is produced in abundance, featuring reds such as those made from excellent Teroldego grapes and the musical Marzemino Gentile—which was worthy of a mention in Mozart's opera *Don Giovanni*—and whites made from the fragrant Gewürztraminer and Müller-Thurgau varieties, among others.

All these flavors are showcased in beautiful village or town squares at festivals or special events dedicated to them; in farmhouses, where some families perpetuate the tradition of "homemade" charcuterie; and in the valleys, where the air makes the best and most environmentally friendly aperitivo. Likewise, when you dine in beautiful rooms decorated with carved wood paneling and heated by elegant majolica-tiled stoves, the arrival of food is worthy of celebration. Just imagine the taste of two slices of dark bread thickly spread with butter to make a speck sandwich, and the sweet softness of plum-filled dumplings.

Barley soup

Also known as *gerstensuppe,* this is a dish of the South Tyrol region, made from pearl barley, vegetables, and smoked pork (speck or pancetta), cooked in meat stock or water and with an unmistakable Alpine flavour.

PREPARATION TIME 15 minutes

COOKING TIME 2 hours

SERVES 4

3½ ounces/100 g speck (cured and smoked ham), cut into small cubes

3½ ounces/½ cup/100 g pearl barley, well washed

50 fl oz/6¼ cups/1.5 liters meat stock (optional)

1 carrot, cut into small pieces

1 celery stalk, cut into small pieces

1 potato, cut into small pieces

1 leek, sliced

1 small onion, sliced

Salt and black pepper

Chopped chives, to garnish

Place the speck in a large saucepan over a medium heat and when the fatty part of the speck turns translucent, add the barley. Stir to combine, add 50 fl oz/6¼ cups/1.5 liters water or meat stock, and simmer for about 1½ hours, stirring occasionally.

Add the carrot, celery, potato, leek, and onion. Season with salt and cook for another 30 minutes.

Remove from the heat and pour the soup into individual bowls or a soup tureen. Serve piping hot garnished with chopped chives.

Trento-style dumplings

There are many variations of this dumpling dish; this recipe is from the province of Trento and is characterized by the use of garlic salami—delicious, delicate, and full of flavor.

PREPARATION TIME 45 minutes
COOKING TIME 1 hour 15 minutes
CHILLING TIME 2–24 hours
SERVES 6

FOR THE VEGETABLE STOCK
1 potato, coarsely chopped
1 onion, coarsely chopped
2 cloves garlic
2 celery stalks, coarsely chopped
2 sprigs parsley
2 carrots, coarsely chopped
1 zucchini (courgette), coarsely chopped
1 piece Parmesan cheese rind
Salt and black pepper

FOR THE DUMPLINGS
1 pound 5 ounces/600 g stale bread
20 fl oz/2½ cups/600 ml milk
3 eggs
2 tablespoons chopped parsley
7 ounces/1⅓ cups/200 g grated aged Vezzena cheese
2 thick slices garlic salami, cut into small pieces
All-purpose (plain) flour, for coating
3 ounces/¾ stick/80 g butter
A few fresh sage leaves

For the vegetable stock, combine all the ingredients in a large saucepan, season with salt and pepper, and cook for about 1 hour. Remove from the heat and set aside to cool.

Meanwhile, for the dumplings, crumble the bread into coarse pieces—they should not be as fine as regular bread crumbs nor in large chunks. Put the bread into a heatproof bowl.

Heat the milk in another large saucepan until warm, pour it onto the bread, and mix with your hands to combine. Set aside to cool.

Add the eggs, chopped parsley, grated cheese, and salami to the cool mixture and season with salt. Refrigerate the mixture for 2–24 hours to let it compact.

Spread a few tablespoons of flour on a plate, or on a cloth (this method is gentler so as not to risk the dumplings falling apart). Using your hands, shape the mixture into roughly egg-size balls, then lightly toss them in the flour until coated.

Heat the vegetable stock in a large saucepan, add the dumplings, a few at a time, and cook for 10–15 minutes until they are cooked through. Remove with a slotted spoon and set aside while you cook the rest.

Melt the butter in a small saucepan, add the sage leaves, and fry for a few minutes. Serve the dumplings with the fried sage and melted butter.

Spinach gnocchi

A specialty of Trentino, this rustic gnocchi dish was invented to make use of leftover bread and the herbs picked in the fields. *Strangolapreti* literally translates as "priest chokers."

PREPARATION TIME 30 minutes
COOKING TIME 20 minutes
SOAKING TIME 30 minutes
SERVES 4

14 ounces/400 g stale bread, crusts removed and cut into cubes
17 fl oz/2 cups/500 ml milk
1 pound 2 ounces/500 g fresh spinach
Extra-virgin olive oil, for sautéing
2 eggs
3½ ounces/1¼ cups/100 g grated hard cheese, such as Parmesan,
  plus extra to serve (optional)
Grated nutmeg, for sprinkling
3½ ounces/generous ¾ cup/100 g Italian "00" flour,
  plus extra if needed
3 ounces/¾ stick/80 g unsalted butter
A few fresh sage leaves
Salt

Place the bread in a large bowl, pour in the milk, and leave to soak for 30 minutes, stirring occasionally so that the milk is completely absorbed.

Meanwhile, cook the spinach in a large saucepan of boiling water for about 5 minutes. Remove the spinach from the pan, set aside to cool, then squeeze the leaves very well to drain. Chop the leaves with a knife. Heat a little extra-virgin olive oil in a large skillet (frying pan), add the spinach, and sauté for 2 minutes.

Squeeze the soaked bread well, then crumble it with your hands or chop it with a knife. Add to a large bowl with the spinach, eggs, grated cheese, a pinch of salt, and a sprinkling of nutmeg and stir everything with a spoon to combine.

Add the flour and mix until combined. It should be compact enough to be used in a pastry (piping) bag. The amount of flour you will need to add may vary slightly depending on how moist the initial mixture is.

Bring plenty of salted water to a boil in a large saucepan. Make the gnocchi by piping 1¼-inch/3-cm-long pieces of the mixture directly into the water. When they float to the top, leave them to cook for a few more minutes.

Meanwhile, melt the butter in a large skillet (frying pan) and add the sage leaves to flavor it. Using a slotted spoon, remove the gnocchi from the cooking water and transfer them to the pan with the melted butter. Swirl the pan to coat the gnocchi in the butter without breaking them. Finish with a sprinkling of grated cheese as desired. Serve immediately.

Coleslaw with speck

Insalata di cavolo
cappuccio e speck

A simple and very appetizing dish of two basic
ingredients—white cabbage and speck (smoked
ham). Caraway seeds are little used in Italian cooking,
but popular in the Trentino-Alto Adige region.

PREPARATION TIME 20 minutes
COOKING TIME 5–8 minutes
SERVES 4

1 medium-small white cabbage, outer tough leaves removed,
  quartered, cored, and shredded
1 level tablespoon caraway seeds
1 tablespoon extra-virgin olive oil
5 ounces/150 g speck (cured and smoked ham), cut into
  cubes or strips
White wine vinegar, for drizzling
Black pepper

Place the cabbage in a salad bowl and season with pepper
and the caraway seeds.

Heat the oil in a large skillet (frying pan) over a low heat,
add the speck, and fry until they are golden all over.
Drizzle with vinegar and cook until it has evaporated, then
pour over the cabbage. Mix well and serve immediately.

Potato cake

A simple, traditional Trentino recipe of oven-baked grated potato, and an ideal vegetarian second course. A perfect example of the *cucina povera* (literally "poor cuisine") culinary style, using locally grown ingredients.

PREPARATION TIME 30 minutes

COOKING TIME 35 minutes

SERVES 6

Olive oil, for greasing
Unsalted butter, in small curls, plus extra for greasing
2 pounds 4 ounces/1 kg potatoes, peeled and grated
1 egg
4 ounces/1 cup/120 g all-purpose (plain) flour
Grated Spressa delle Giudicarie cheese, for sprinkling
Salt and black pepper
Coleslaw or cheese, to serve

Preheat the oven to 375 °F/190 °C/170 °C Fan/Gas 5. Grease a 9½-inch/24-cm round cake pan (tin) with oil and butter.

Place the grated potatoes in a large bowl. Add the egg and flour, season with salt and pepper, and mix well, adding 7 fl oz/scant 1 cup/200 ml water, a little at a time, until it is all incorporated.

Spoon the mixture into the prepared pan, top with the grated cheese and butter curls, and bake in the preheated oven for about 35 minutes until golden brown on top. Remove from the oven, leave to rest for 5 minutes, then turn out into a serving dish. Serve with coleslaw or cheese.

Venison in blueberry sauce

The blueberry sauce in this dish works wonderfully with the strong taste of the venison—the roe deer is found in vast numbers across the region, and seasonal game dishes are a specialty.

PREPARATION TIME 30 minutes
COOKING TIME 2 hours
MARINATING TIME 24 hours
SERVES 4

2 pounds 4 ounces/1 kg boned leg or shoulder of venison,
   cut into small pieces
1 onion, chopped
1 carrot, chopped
1 celery stalk, chopped
3 dried bay leaves
4 juniper berries
Pinch of marjoram
1 bottle (25 fl oz/750 ml) red wine
2¾ fl oz/⅓ cup/80 ml olive oil
7 ounces/200 g salted pancetta, chopped
All-purpose (plain) flour, for dusting
7 ounces/1⅔ cups/200 g blueberries (fresh or frozen)
3½ fl oz/scant ½ cup/100 ml heavy (double) cream
Salt and black pepper

Place the venison in a large bowl with the chopped vegetables, bay leaves, juniper, and marjoram and mix well to combine. Pour in the wine, cover with plastic wrap (cling film), and leave to marinate in the refrigerator for 24 hours.

After 24 hours, remove the meat and vegetables from the marinade and set aside. Strain the marinade through a fine-mesh strainer (sieve) into a large bowl or jug and set aside.

Heat the oil in a large saucepan with a lid or terracotta cooking pot over a medium heat, add the chopped pancetta, and cook for 10 minutes. Meanwhile, spread the flour out on a large plate, add the meat, and toss until it is lightly coated all over. Add the meat to the pan and brown it in the oil with the pancetta. Add the marinated vegetables and cook for a few more minutes, then add the strained marinade. Season with salt and pepper, cover with a lid, and cook for 1½ hours.

Remove the meat from the pan and keep it warm. Add the blueberries to the cooking liquid and gently simmer for 5 minutes. Strain the sauce through a fine-mesh strainer and return it to the pan. Add the stewed meat and cream, heat through, and serve immediately.

Walnut strudel

Walnuts are often found in desserts in the northern Italian regions, and this is a rustic-style, wintry dish with a soft, sweet filling of walnuts and honey encased in pastry.

PREPARATION TIME 30 minutes

COOKING TIME 30 minutes

RESTING TIME 1 hour

SERVES 6

FOR THE PASTRY

9 ounces/2 cups/250 g all-purpose (plain) flour, plus extra
   for dusting
1 egg
2 tablespoons vegetable oil
Pinch of salt

FOR THE FILLING

7 ounces/1½ cups/200 g shelled walnuts
3½ fl oz/scant ½ cup/100 ml whole milk
5 ounces/½ cup/150 g honey
Grated zest of 1 lemon

TO FINISH

1 egg yolk
1 tablespoon whole milk

For the pastry, gather all the ingredients on a clean work surface and mix, then knead to a smooth and soft dough, adding a little lukewarm water only if necessary. Heat a large heatproof bowl by filling it with boiling water. Empty and dry it and place it upturned over the dough to cover it completely. Leave to rest for about 1 hour.

Preheat the oven to 350 °F/180 °C/160 °C Fan/Gas 4.

For the filling, mix the walnuts with the milk, honey, and lemon zest in a large bowl until fully combined.

Roll out the dough on a very lightly floured work surface with a rolling pin to a ¼-inch/5-mm thickness. Place the dough on a kitchen cloth and stretch the edges with your fingertips so the edges of the pastry are thinner, taking care not to break it. Spread the walnut filling on top, then using the cloth to help you, roll up the dough into a log.

To finish, mix the egg yolk and a little milk together in a small bowl. Line a baking pan (tin) with dampened parchment paper. Lay the strudel on it and bend it gently into a horseshoe shape, then brush the pastry all over with the egg wash. Bake in the preheated oven for about 30 minutes, or until golden brown.

Remove the strudel from the oven and leave to rest for 5 minutes, then transfer it to a serving dish and serve sliced either warm or at room temperature.

"Imperial mess"

Kaiserschmarren means "imperial mess," in reference to the accidental creation of a shredded pancake by the chef of Emperor Franz Joseph of neighboring Austria. A hearty afternoon treat served with jam.

PREPARATION TIME 10 minutes

COOKING TIME 15–20 minutes

SOAKING TIME 20 minutes

SERVES 4

2 ounces/¼ cup/50 g raisins

Rum, for soaking

7 ounces/1⅔ cups/200 g all-purpose (plain) flour

10 fl oz/1¼ cups/300 ml whole milk

1 teaspoon salt

1 ounce/2½ tablespoons/30 g superfine (caster) sugar

3 eggs, separated

2¼ ounces/½ stick/60 g unsalted butter

Confectioners' (icing) sugar, for caramelizing

Blueberry jam, to serve

Place the raisins in a small bowl, add enough rum to cover, and leave to soak for at least 20 minutes.

Place the flour, milk, salt, superfine (caster) sugar, and egg yolks in a large bowl and mix to a smooth batter. Beat the egg whites in another bowl with an electric whisk or in a stand mixer fitted with a whisk attachment to stiff peaks, then fold them into the batter, taking care not to let them collapse.

Drain the raisins and add them to the batter. Heat a large skillet (frying pan) until hot, then add 2 tablespoons of the butter and allow to melt. Add the batter to the skillet to make a pancake, about ½ inch/1 cm thick, and cook until the pancake is golden brown on both sides. Using a spatula, coarsely shred the pancake, then add the remaining butter and some confectioners' (icing) sugar and cook until it is caramelized. Serve immediately with blueberry jam.

Veneto

The many different degrees of softness

The Veneto is an extraordinary land where *ombra* ("shadow") means a glass of wine and *cicchetti* is the local variant of tapas, where sardines are paired with raisins (page 94) and onions go wonderfully with liver. It is where a dried cod (stockfish) is turned very soft, almost to a cream (page 98). It is where the consistency of steaming pasta e fasioi (page 97) is constantly checked until the wooden spoon can stand in the middle of the pot, as opposed to the wonderful risi e bisi (page 103), which is arranged on the plate like a wave on the shoreline. It is where the Asiago plateau gifts us with its namesake cheese, and it is home to Montasio, a cheese created by the wise Benedictine monks of Moggio Abbey. The plains of the Veneto region abound with unique vegetables, such as the variously colored radicchio varieties of Treviso, Castelfranco, and Chioggia, and the delicate, creamy hearts of the artichokes grown in the gardens on islands in the Venetian lagoon.

The cuisine of Veneto still tastes of the countryside, with pots of polenta as soft pillows for necklaces made of sausages, poultry crowns, and fish stews, with geese, chickens, and pigeons artfully simmering in pans. Then, when the moment comes to raise a glass, here is King Amarone, a solemn and velvety red wine from Valpolicella; and here is Prince Prosecco, a whitish-gold sparkling wine from Valdobbiadene, served with a soft slice of the sweet pandoro bread traditionally eaten at Christmas.

Sweet and sour sardines

A classic Venetian dish, *saòr* means "taste," and here the fried sardines are laid to rest for 24 hours in a marinade of braised onions, red wine vinegar, and oil, allowing them to absorb all the various flavors.

PREPARATION TIME 40 minutes

COOKING TIME 30 minutes

RESTING TIME 24 hours

SERVES 6

12 fresh sardines
All-purpose (plain) flour, for dusting
Olive oil, for frying
Salt

FOR THE MARINADE
3 tablespoons extra-virgin olive oil
2 medium white onions, sliced
3 tablespoons red wine vinegar
1 tablespoon black peppercorns
2 ounces/generous ⅓ cup/50 g toasted pine nuts (optional)
2 ounces/generous ⅓ cup/50 g raisins, soaked in 2½ fl oz/
  ⅓ cup/75 ml white wine for 1 hour (optional)

Prepare the sardines by scaling, removing the head, gutting, and washing them well under cold running water. Season them lightly with salt and dust with flour. Heat a few tablespoons of oil in a large skillet (frying pan), add the sardines in batches, and fry for 2 minutes on each side. Remove each batch from the pan and drain on paper towels.

For the marinade, heat the oil in a skillet over low–medium heat, add the sliced onions, and sauté for 20 minutes.

Pour in the vinegar, stir to remove all the crispy bits from the bottom of the pan, then remove the pan from the heat. Add the peppercorns with the pine nuts and raisins, if using. Pour half the mixture into a large serving dish, lay six sardines on top, and spread a third of the remaining mixture over them. Lay the remaining six sardines on top and pour over the remaining mixture. Leave to cool, then cover with plastic wrap (cling film) and chill in the refrigerator overnight. Serve the next day at room temperature.

Pasta and beans

A rustic-style dish of maltagliati ("badly cut") pasta, in a hearty soup-style dish typical of the Veneto region, particularly during the winter months. The beans are soaked overnight, so leave plenty of time to prepare.

PREPARATION TIME 30 minutes

COOKING TIME 2 hours 40 minutes

SOAKING TIME 12 hours

SERVES 4

14 ounces/2¼ cups/400 g dried white beans

3 tablespoons extra-virgin olive oil, plus extra to serve

4 fresh sage leaves

1 clove garlic, crushed

3 tablespoons finely chopped tomatoes

3 ounces/80 g egg maltagliati pasta

Salt and black pepper

Soak the beans in a large bowl of water overnight. The next day, drain and cook them in a large saucepan of water for 2 hours, or until tender. Drain the beans, transfer half of them to a blender or food processor, and blend to a purée. Set the other beans aside.

Heat the oil in a large saucepan, add the sage and crushed garlic, and fry for 2 minutes. Add the puréed beans, about 50 fl oz/6 cups/1.5 liters water, and the chopped tomatoes. Season sparingly with salt and cook for 30 minutes.

Add the whole beans followed by the pasta and cook for about 10 minutes. The bean mixture should have quite a thick consistency. Remove from the heat and adjust the seasoning with salt and pepper.

Serve the pasta e fasioi hot, warm, or cold—the dish is delicious any which way—and always with a drizzle of oil.

Creamed cod

A specialty of the Veneto region, the recipe only calls for a handful of ingredients, but the key is in creating a creamy emulsion of the perfect spreadable consistency from the softened cod and the oil.

PREPARATION TIME 40 minutes
COOKING TIME 15–20 minutes
SOAKING TIME 24 hours
SERVES 4

10½ ounces/300 g dried cod (stockfish)
Juice of ½ lemon
1 clove garlic, peeled and left whole
1 dried bay leaf
10 fl oz/1¼ cups/300 ml extra-virgin olive oil
1 cold polenta loaf (store-bought or homemade), cut into slices
1 sprig parsley, chopped, to garnish

Soak the cod (stockfish) in a large bowl of water in the refrigerator for at least 24 hours, changing the water several times. Drain and pat dry with paper towels.

Place the cod into a large saucepan of water. Add the lemon juice, garlic, and bay leaf and bring to a boil. Cook for 15–20 minutes, then drain and transfer the fish to a chopping board. Peel off the skin and remove any bones. Coarsely chop the fish, then put it into a stand mixer fitted with a paddle attachment and start beating while adding the oil in a thin, steady stream until an emulsion similar to mayonnaise is formed.

Meanwhile, heat a griddle or large skillet (frying pan) and, when hot, add the polenta slices, and cook until the slices are brown on both sides.

Spread the creamed cod over the polenta slices and serve garnished with chopped parsley.

Pan-fried artichoke bottoms

Complemented by garlic, parsley, and lemon juice, this Venetian-style side dish is perfect alongside a main dish of meat. Artichoke bottoms can be bought pre-prepared to avoid a laborious preparation process.

PREPARATION TIME 15 minutes

COOKING TIME 20 minutes

SERVES 4

12 artichoke bottoms
Juice of 1 lemon
1¾ fl oz/scant ¼ cup/50 ml olive oil
1 clove garlic, finely chopped
2 tablespoons chopped parsley
1¾ fl oz/scant ¼ cup/50 ml vegetable stock
Salt and black pepper

Place the artichoke bottoms into a large bowl and cover with cold water and the lemon juice.

Heat the oil in a large saucepan with a lid, add the garlic and parsley, and sauté for a few minutes. Drain the artichokes well and add them to the pan. Pour in the stock and stir to scrape up any crispy bits off the bottom of the pan, then season with salt and pepper. Cover the pan with a lid and cook over a medium heat for 10–15 minutes.

Transfer the artichokes to a serving dish and serve hot. They are also delicious simply boiled and seasoned with olive oil, lemon juice, and salt, or with a spicier sauce.

Black rice with cuttlefish

For such a dramatic-looking dish, this is very simple to make. Creamy and soft like a risotto, with a taste of the sea from the ink sacs, it pairs well with a glass of dry white wine.

PREPARATION TIME 20 minutes
COOKING TIME 1 hour
SERVES 8

8 small cuttlefish
2 tablespoons olive oil
1 small onion, finely chopped
1 clove garlic, peeled and left whole
34 fl oz/4 cups/1 liter chicken stock, brought to a boil
1½–2 ounces/3–3½ tablespoons/40–50 g unsalted butter
1 pound 2 ounces/2¾ cups/500 g Carnaroli rice
3 tablespoons finely chopped parsley

Gently remove the ink sacs from the cuttlefish and set three aside. Remove the cuttlebone and cut the cuttlefish into very thin slices.

Heat the oil in a medium saucepan, add the chopped onion and the garlic clove, and sauté for about 5 minutes. Add the cuttlefish and cook for about 30 minutes, adding a few tablespoons of the stock, if necessary. Remove and discard the garlic.

Melt the butter in a large, shallow pan, add the rice, and stir for 3–4 minutes until it turns translucent. Add the stock, one ladleful at a time, and cook, stirring, for 15 minutes. Add the cuttlefish and the three ink sacs. Continue to cook while stirring and adding stock for another 5 minutes, until all the stock is used up and the rice is al dente.

Remove the pan from the heat and sprinkle over the parsley. Transfer to a serving dish and serve.

Bigoli in anchovy sauce

A typical starter dish of the Veneto, with anchovies as the star and creating a creamy sauce for the bigoli pasta, a thicker form of spaghetti. This dish is traditionally served on the Feast of the Redeemer in July.

PREPARATION TIME 15 minutes

COOKING TIME 20 minutes

SOAKING TIME 5–20 minutes

SERVES 4

3½ ounces/100 g salt-packed anchovies
2 tablespoons olive oil
1 white onion, thinly sliced
11 ounces/320 g bigoli pasta
Salt

Soak the anchovies in a bowl of water for 5–20 minutes, then drain, remove any bones, and divide the fillets with your hands. Set them aside.

To make the sauce, heat the oil in a large skillet (frying pan), add the onion, and cook for 15–20 minutes, adding a few tablespoons of water until soft. Add the anchovies and stir carefully so that they break down completely, creating a creamy texture.

Meanwhile, cook the pasta in a large saucepan of boiling salted water until al dente. Drain and stir the pasta into the sauce to coat well. Serve.

Rice and peas

A creamy, thick, soup-style dish of rice and peas, made using the freshest spring peas found in the region. The local rice is called Vialone Nano Veronese (PGI), though Arborio and Carnaroli will work in the dish too.

PREPARATION TIME 20 minutes

COOKING TIME 1 hour

SERVES 4

1 pound 12 ounces/800 g fresh peas
2 tablespoons olive oil
2 ounces/50 g lean pancetta or cured ham, finely chopped
½ onion, finely chopped
10½ ounces/1¾ cups/300 g risotto rice (see headnote)
34 fl oz/4¼ cups/1 liter chicken or vegetable stock
Salt and black pepper
Chopped parsley, to serve
1½ ounces/½ cup/40 g grated Parmesan cheese, to serve

Shell the peas and set them aside. Wash the pods, then cook them in a large saucepan of boiling salted water for 30 minutes. Purée them through a food mill or in a blender to a runny consistency.

Heat the oil in a large saucepan, add the pancetta and onion, and sauté for 5 minutes. Add the rice, mix well, then add the pea-pod purée and stir gently to mix. Cook for another 5 minutes, then add the shelled peas. Stir, add a ladleful of stock, and cook until the rice is quite soft, thick, and creamy, adding the stock a ladleful at a time until it is all used up. Adjust the seasoning with salt and pepper, and serve with chopped parsley and grated Parmesan cheese.

Grilled Treviso radicchio

Radicchio di Treviso in gratella

A quick, easy, and tasty side for meats, this strikingly colorful dish is traditionally made using Radicchio Rosso di Treviso (PGI), a variety of chicory grown in Treviso, Padua, and Venice.

PREPARATION TIME 20 minutes

COOKING TIME 10 minutes

SERVES 4

4 heads radicchio, either left whole or halved, depending on size
Olive oil, for brushing and drizzling
Salt and black pepper

Brush the radicchio with plenty of oil and season with salt and pepper.

Light a barbecue or preheat the broiler (grill).

Arrange the radicchio either on a grill grate or oven rack and cook them for 5 minutes on each side until wilted and lightly charred. Transfer to a serving dish, drizzle with oil, season with salt if needed, and serve.

Tiramisu

One of the most famous desserts in all of Italy, it has spawned numerous variations across the world, but the traditional recipe contains eggs, mascarpone, ladyfingers (sponge fingers), and coffee.

PREPARATION TIME 20 minutes

CHILLING TIME 3 hours

SERVES 6

2 egg whites

4 egg yolks

5 ounces/1½ cups/150 g confectioners' (icing) sugar

14 ounces/1¾ cups/400 g mascarpone

7 ounces/200 g savoiardi ladyfingers (sponge fingers)

25 fl oz/3 cups/750 ml ristretto coffee (highly concentrated espresso coffee)

7 ounces/200 g dark chocolate, grated

Unsweetened cocoa powder, for dusting

Using an electric whisk, beat the egg whites to stiff peaks in a large bowl.

Combine the egg yolks and sugar in another bowl and whisk until pale and fluffy. Fold the mascarpone into the mixture, then gently fold in the beaten egg whites.

Cover the bottom of a deep rectangular serving dish, approximately 10½ × 8½ inches (27 × 22 cm), with a layer of ladyfingers (sponge fingers) and carefully brush them with the coffee. Alternatively, gently dip them into the coffee without allowing too much to soak in and arrange them in the dish.

Cover the ladyfingers with a layer of mascarpone cream and dust it with a little grated chocolate. Repeat until all the ingredients are used up, finishing with a layer of mascarpone dusted with cocoa powder. Chill in the refrigerator for at least 3 hours before serving.

Grappa and lemon pastries

Galani, also known as *crostoli* in the Veneto region, are deep-fried strips of dough dusted with confectioners' (icing) sugar, flavored with grappa, white wine, and lemon, and typically served during Carnival.

PREPARATION TIME 45 minutes

COOKING TIME 15 minutes

RESTING TIME 30 minutes

SERVES 6–8

1 pound 2 ounces/generous 4 cups/500 g Italian "00" flour

1 egg

2 egg yolks

¾ ounce/heaping 1 tablespoon/25 g unsalted butter, cubed

4 tablespoons superfine (caster) sugar

2 teaspoons baking powder

Grated zest of 1 lemon

Pinch of salt

20 ml grappa

4–4½ fl oz/½–generous ½ cup/120–130 ml white wine

Peanut (groundnut) oil, for deep-frying

Confectioners' (icing) sugar, for dusting

Combine the flour, egg, yolks, butter, superfine (caster) sugar, baking powder, grated lemon zest, the salt, and the grappa in a large bowl or on a clean work surface. Mix with your fingertips until crumbly, then add the wine and mix to form a dough. Knead the dough until it is soft, smooth, and compact, then gather into a ball, wrap in plastic wrap (cling film), and leave to rest at room temperature for 30 minutes.

Take a small piece of dough (leaving the remainder wrapped) and roll it through a pasta machine, gradually adjusting the thickness with each pass until the sheet is ¹⁄₁₆ inch/2 mm thick. Using a fluted pastry wheel, trim the edges of the pasta sheet and cut it into small rectangles. Make a diagonal cut in the center of each rectangle, without going to the edges. Repeat the process until you have run out of dough.

Heat enough oil for deep-frying in a large, deep saucepan to 340 °F/170 °C on a thermometer, or until a cube of bread browns in 30 seconds. Carefully add a few of the galani at a time, starting with the first ones that were cut out, and deep-fry for 3 minutes, or until golden brown. Using a slotted spoon, remove them from the oil and drain on paper towels. Dust them with confectioners' (icing) sugar and serve immediately.

Friuli-Venezia Giulia

More than 130 flavors of tradition

The evolution of the cuisine of Friuli-Venezia Giulia has not distorted the traditional flavors of the once-poor mountain region, instead enhancing them and making them compatible with current tastes. The rich Austro-Hungarian influence has also been incorporated through simplification. As a result, the region boasts more than 130 foods that are listed as "traditional," starting with the exquisite San Daniele, Cormons, and Sauris prosciutto. And while the Alpine Carnia region is home to Montasio cheese, with its protected designation of origin status and different levels of maturity, many others, known as *malga* (mountain pasture) and *latteria* (dairy) cheeses, with their pleasant contrasts of spicy notes and sweet creaminess, fortunately also reach the lowlands. This cuisine is quite surprising because, despite its rustic simplicity, it offers a wide range of truly unusual flavors, including hearty soups with grains and vegetables, legumes (pulses) and cured meats, the daring combination of cotechini sausages and pickled turnips, and succulent and tender goose, which has been revived with great success. And while the Venezia Giulia side of the region offers fish and seafood from the coast in an impressive mix of soups and shellfish dishes, Friuli, which boasts 20,000 hectares of magnificent vineyards, each year produces 100 million bottles of extraordinary wines, such as Refosco, Terrano, Friulano (formerly Tocai), Ribolla Gialla, Pinot Bianco, and Pinot Grigio, which make winters less cold and summers cooler.

Spider crab taglierini

Spider crabs (*granceola*) are found along the coastline of Friuli-Venezia Giulia and contain large amounts of white meat. Here they are paired with fresh taglierini for a delicious pasta dish.

PREPARATION TIME 45 minutes

COOKING TIME 1 hour

SERVES 4

1 spider crab, about 1 pound 9 ounces–1 pound
   12 ounces/700–800 g
4 tablespoons vegetable oil
2 tablespoons unsalted butter
1 clove garlic
1 shot glass brandy, about ¾ fl oz/4 teaspoons/25ml
10 ounces/280 g fresh taglierini
Salt and white pepper

For the sauce, place the spider crab in a large saucepan, cover with water, and bring to a boil. Boil for 20–30 minutes, then drain, detach its legs and pincers and set aside, and pry open its body beneath its eyes.

Remove all the white meat (use kitchen tweezers to help with this task), eggs if any (orange in color and found in clusters), and the pieces of brown meat, and put everything into a large bowl. Carefully remove the meat from the legs and pincers.

To make a crab stock, put the reserved spider crab legs and pincers into a large saucepan with 17 fl oz/2 cups/500 ml water and bring to a boil. Boil about 20 minutes, then strain the stock through a fine-mesh strainer (sieve) into another bowl, adjusting the seasoning sparingly with salt.

Heat the oil and butter in a small saucepan. Add the garlic and sauté until golden, then remove and discard. Stir in the crab meat, add the brandy, and allow it to evaporate. Pour in 3½ fl oz/scant ½ cup/100 ml of the crab stock and cook until the stock has reduced slightly. Adjust the seasoning with salt.

Meanwhile, cook the pasta in a large saucepan of boiling salted water for 10 minutes, or until al dente. Drain and arrange the pasta in a serving dish. Coat with the crab sauce, season with a sprinkling or two of white pepper, and serve piping hot.

Springtime ravioli

Every village in the Carnia area of the region has its own version of this traditional Friulian first course of sweet yet slightly savory ravioli-style pasta filled with ricotta, herbs, and raisins.

PREPARATION TIME 1 hour 15 minutes
COOKING TIME 10–15 minutes
RESTING TIME 3 hours
MAKES ABOUT 60

10½ ounces/2½ cups/300 g all-purpose (plain) flour
2 ounces/3½ tablespoons/50 g unsalted butter, plus
   5½ ounces/1¼ sticks/150 g unsalted butter, melted
7 ounces/scant 1 cup/200 g ricotta affumicata cheese
1 tablespoon chopped chives
Salt

FOR THE FILLING
2 ounces/⅓ cup/50 g raisins
1¾ fl oz/scant ¼ cup/50 ml rum
10½ ounces/1¼ cups/300 g fresh ricotta cheese
2 tablespoons unsalted butter
½ sachet (about 4 g) vanilla sugar

A small handful of fresh herbs (lemon balm, peppermint, parsley, marjoram, oak-leaved geranium, lemon thyme), chopped
1 small apple, preferably Reinette, cored and diced
2 ounces/50 g dry cookies (biscuits), crumbled
1 tablespoon cherry or strawberry jam
Pinch of ground cinnamon
Grated zest of 1 lemon
2 ounces/generous ⅓ cup/50 g chopped walnuts

To make the filling, place the raisins in a small bowl, add the rum, and leave to soak for 10–15 minutes.

Meanwhile, combine the ricotta with the butter in a large saucepan over a low heat, add the vanilla sugar, and allow some of its moisture to evaporate. Stir in the chopped herbs and cook for 5 minutes.

Drain the rum-soaked raisins and squeeze them out. Chop half of them and mix them all with the ricotta, diced apple, crumbled cookies (biscuits), jam, cinnamon, lemon zest, and the walnuts. Set aside to rest for 2 hours.

For the pasta, gather the flour into a mound on a clean work surface and make a well in the center. Heat 1¾ fl oz/scant ¼ cup/50 ml water in a small saucepan, add the 2 ounces/3½ tablespoons/50 g butter, and

leave to melt, then pour the hot mixture into the well and add a little salt. Mix and knead until it is a smooth dough. Wrap in plastic wrap (cling film) and leave to rest for 1 hour.

Roll out the dough into a thin sheet. Using a 2¾-inch/ 7-cm cookie cutter, cut out as many small disks as possible. Place a teaspoon of the filling in the center of each disk, brush the edges with cold water, fold the disk over, and seal the edges.

Bring a large saucepan of water to a boil, add the cialsòns in batches, and cook until they float to the top. Remove them with a slotted spoon to a bowl, then sprinkle them with half of the cheese, all the chives, and then the remaining cheese. Finally, pour over the melted butter and serve.

Trieste-style sauerkraut and bean soup

Perfect winter comfort food and one of the best-known dishes of Trieste, this is a hearty, rustic soup of beans, sauerkraut, and pork ribs, thought to have its origins in Slovenia and Croatia.

PREPARATION TIME 15 minutes

COOKING TIME 3 hours

SOAKING TIME 12 hours

SERVES 6

9 ounces/generous 1⅓ cups/250 g dried beans, such as cranberry (borlotti)
2 potatoes
1 onion, sliced (optional)
1 dried bay leaf
2 cloves garlic, peeled and left whole
7 ounces/200 g pork ribs
4 tablespoons olive oil
2 tablespoons all-purpose (plain) flour
3½ ounces/100 g smoked pancetta, thickly sliced
9 ounces/250 g sauerkraut
Salt and black pepper

Soak the beans in a large bowl of cold water for 12 hours.

The next day, drain the beans and put them into a large saucepan with the whole potatoes, sliced onion, if using, bay leaf, 1 garlic clove, and the pork ribs. Pour in 50 fl oz/6 cups/1.5 liters cold water, place over a low heat, and simmer for about 1 hour.

Meanwhile, heat 2 tablespoons of the oil in a small pan over a medium heat. Finely chop the remaining garlic clove, add to the pan, and sauté briefly. Stir in the flour and cook until the mixture has turned a nutty brown color. Add this mixture to the beans and cook for another 30 minutes.

Heat the remaining oil in another saucepan with a lid, add the pancetta, and cook for a few minutes. Add the sauerkraut, season with salt and pepper, cover with a lid, and cook over a low heat for about 1 hour 30 minutes, stirring occasionally. Add a little hot water if the sauerkraut dries out too much.

When the sauerkraut is cooked, add it to the beans, adjust the seasoning with salt and pepper, and cook for another 20 minutes. Remove the pan from the heat, leave the soup to rest at room temperature, then serve lukewarm.

Stewed turnips

Turnips are an essential ingredient in Friulian cuisine, grown in abundance across the region, and harvested in the fall. Here they are cooked in butter, sugar, and stock in a simple peasant-style dish.

PREPARATION TIME 20 minutes

COOKING TIME 20 minutes

SERVES 6

1½ ounces/3 tablespoons/40 g unsalted butter

½ ounce/4 teaspoons/15 g superfine (caster) sugar

2 pounds 4 ounces/1 kg fresh turnips, unpeeled and cut into uniform pieces

Vegetable stock, for moistening

Salt and black pepper

Melt the butter and sugar together in a large saucepan. When the sugar starts to caramelize, add the turnips, and stir to coat well. Cover the pan and cook over a low heat for 10 minutes, or until the turnips are tender. Uncover and taste and adjust the seasoning with salt and pepper. If necessary, add a little stock to soften the contents of the pan before serving.

Scampi in tomatoes and white wine

A dish of Dalmatian influence, the origin of the term *bùzara* is disputed, and is thought to refer either to the cooking pots used by fishermen on their boats, or the tomato and wine "stew" that surrounds the scampi.

PREPARATION TIME 15 minutes

COOKING TIME 20 minutes

SERVES 8

1 tablespoon tomato paste (purée)
6 tablespoons vegetable oil
1 onion, thinly sliced
2–3 cloves garlic, peeled and left whole
24 large scampi (langoustines), shelled
Generous splash of dry white wine
3–4 tablespoons bread crumbs
2 tablespoons chopped parsley
Salt and black pepper

Add the tomato paste (purée) to a cup or small bowl and dilute with a little hot water.

Heat the oil in a large saucepan with a lid, add the onion, and sauté for 10 minutes. Add the garlic and sauté until they turn golden, then remove and discard them.

Add the scampi to the pan and stir gently until they color. Add the tomato paste and the wine, cover, and cook for 3–4 minutes, shaking the pan frequently.

Sprinkle the bread crumbs over the scampi and cook for 1–2 minutes. Taste and adjust the seasoning with salt and pepper. Remove from the heat, transfer the scampi to a serving dish, sprinkle with the chopped parsley, and serve immediately.

Trieste-style cod

Simple ingredients have over time become an exquisite regional delicacy, with layers of air-dried cod (stockfish) and potato interspersed with the flavors of anchovy and parsley.

PREPARATION TIME 30 minutes
COOKING TIME 1 hour
SERVES 4

2 pounds 4 ounces/1 kg cod (stockfish) fillet, soaked and drained
1 pound 12 ounces/800 g potatoes, peeled and cut into thin slices
3½ ounces/100 g oil-packed anchovy fillets, cut into small pieces
2 tablespoons finely chopped parsley
Extra-virgin olive oil, plus extra for greasing and drizzling
Salt

Remove the skin and any bones from the fish and cut the flesh into pieces as uniform in size as possible.

Preheat the oven to 350 °F/180 °C/160 °C Fan/Gas 4.

Add the anchovies to a bowl with some of the chopped parsley, then add the oil, and mix well to make a sauce. Set aside.

Grease the bottom and sides of a large ovenproof dish with 2–3 tablespoons oil and arrange half the potato slices slightly overlapped in a radial pattern. Add a layer of sauce, cover it with cod pieces, sprinkle with chopped parsley, and drizzle with oil. Arrange the remaining potatoes over the cod, season with sauce, and moisten everything with a ladleful of water (taking care not to wash off the sauce).

Bake in the preheated oven for about 1 hour, or until the potatoes are soft and golden. Remove and leave the dish to rest for a short while before serving.

Cheese and potato cake

Frico is a crispy-topped potato cake with a soft, cheesy center. Montasio cheese (PDO) is a regional specialty—a cooked-curd, semi-hard cheese with a mild and delicate flavor.

PREPARATION TIME 20 minutes
COOKING TIME 35–40 minutes
SERVES 4

1 tablespoon extra-virgin olive oil
1 pound 2 ounces/500 g red-skinned potatoes, peeled and
    coarsely grated
1 pound 2 ounces/generous 4 cups/500 g grated Montasio
    cheese, preferably a mix of young and more sharp
    (mature) varieties
Salt and black pepper

Heat the oil in a large skillet (frying pan) over a low heat, add the potatoes, and stir and cook for 10–15 minutes until soft. Add the cheese and season with salt and pepper. Mix very well until all ingredients are thoroughly combined. Increase the heat to medium-low and continue to cook, stirring occasionally. When the cheese has melted completely, increase the heat slightly and cook until a golden crust forms on the bottom. Using a plate or pan lid, turn the frico over like an omelet and cook the other side until the same crust forms. Transfer to a plate, cut it into slices, and serve.

Easter fruit and chocolate pastry

A specialty of Trieste, and served primarily at Easter, this festive spiral-shaped puff pastry dessert is filled with dried fruits, nuts, chocolate, and a generous amount of alcohol!

PREPARATION TIME 40 minutes
COOKING TIME 30 minutes
CHILLING TIME 17 hours; SOAKING TIME 30 minutes
SERVES 6

FOR THE DOUGH
7 ounces/1⅔ cups/200 g all-purpose (plain) flour, plus extra for dusting
1 egg yolk
1½ ounces/3 tablespoons/40 g unsalted butter, softened
1 tablespoon extra-virgin olive oil
Pinch of salt

FOR THE BEURRAGE
4 ounces/1 stick/115 g unsalted butter
2 ounces/scant ½ cup/50 g all-purpose (plain) flour

FOR THE FILLING
3½ ounces/¾ cup/100 g raisins
1¾ fl oz/scant ¼ cup/50 ml Commandaria dessert wine
1¾ fl oz/scant ¼ cup/50 ml Moscato wine
2–3 tablespoons Maraschino liqueur
1 tablespoon rum
1 tablespoon Cointreau
6 ounces/1½ sticks/180 g unsalted butter, plus extra for greasing
9 ounces/scant 2 cups/250 g chopped walnuts
4 ounces/1 cup/120 g chopped almonds
4 ounces/scant 1 cup/120 g pine nuts
4 ounces/scant 1 cup/120 g chopped candied citrón peel
10½ ounces/300 g chocolate, coarsely chopped
5½ ounces/¾ cup/160 g superfine (caster) sugar
Grated zest and juice of 1 orange
Vanilla extract, to taste

TO FINISH
Unsalted butter, melted and cooled
1–2 egg yolks, mixed with a little water

For the dough, gather the flour into a mound on a work surface and make a well in the center. Add the egg yolk, butter, oil, 3½ fl oz/scant ½ cup/100 ml cold water, and the salt to the well, then mix and knead until smooth. Wrap in plastic wrap (cling film) and refrigerate.

To make the beurrage, place the butter and flour in a small bowl and mix together to combine. Shape the mixture into a block, wrap it in plastic wrap, and refrigerate for 2 hours.

Roll out the chilled dough and use it to encase the chilled butter block, then roll out and fold the pastry six times, turning it 90 degrees each time. Leave the pastry to rest for 2 hours wrapped in a dry cloth and then a damp cloth. Finally, place it between two soup plates and refrigerate for 12 hours.

For the filling, place the raisins in a bowl, pour in all the alcohol, and leave to soak for 30 minutes. Grease a large baking sheet with butter and add a dusting of flour.

Add the remaining filling ingredients to the raisins and mix to combine. Divide the dough in half and roll each half out into a disk. Place them on kitchen cloths dusted with flour and brush them with cooled melted butter. Spread the filling on top, roll them up into a log, and seal the ends, then roll each log into a coil. Arrange the pastry coils on the prepared baking sheet, brush all over with the egg yolk, and. refrigerate for 30 minutes.

Preheat the oven to 400 °F/200 °C/180 °C Fan/Gas 6, and bake the pastries for 30 minutes. Remove them from the oven and set aside to cool before serving.

Celebration fruit and nut cake

A close relation of the presnitz (page 123), the gubana has its origins in the Natisone river valley on the border of Friuli and Slovenia, and is served at Christmas and Easter, and at family weddings and christenings.

PREPARATION TIME 45 minutes
COOKING TIME 1 hour 20 minutes
RESTING TIME 26 hours
SERVES 6

8 ounces/generous 1¾ cups/220 g all-purpose (plain) flour
¼ ounce/10 g fresh yeast
1½ fl oz/3 tablespoons/40 ml milk, warmed
2 ounces/scant ¼ cup/50 g superfine (caster) sugar
1 egg, plus 1 ounce/30 g egg yolk, plus 1 egg white, lightly beaten
2¼ ounces/½ stick/60 g unsalted butter, softened
Salt

FOR THE FILLING
2 ounces/¼ cup/60 g superfine (caster) sugar
Dash of white wine vinegar

5 ounces/1 cup/140 g shelled walnuts
¾ ounce/heaping 1 tablespoon/20 g unsalted butter
1 ounce/scant ¼ cup/30 g pine nuts
1½ ounces/40 g amaretti biscuits
1 ounce/30 g biscotti biscuits
2¼ ounces/scant ½ cup/60 g raisins, soaked in rum
Grated zest of ½ lemon
Vanilla extract and ground cinnamon, to taste
¾ ounce/scant ¼ cup/20 g candied citron, chopped (optional)
Plum brandy (Slivovitz), for moistening

For the filling, in a heavy bottomed saucepan, add half the sugar, 1 tablespoon water, and the vinegar, and cook until caramelized. Add one-third of the walnuts and stir for a few seconds. Transfer the mixture to an oiled work surface, and set aside to cool.

Meanwhile, melt the butter in a skillet (frying pan) over a very low heat, add the pine nuts, and roast until golden. Remove from the heat and set aside to cool.

Chop the amaretti and biscotti biscuits, the caramelized walnuts, and the remaining walnuts into very small pieces. Transfer to a large bowl. Drain the raisins and squeeze well, then add to the bowl with the roasted pine nuts and butter, grated lemon zest, a pinch of salt, vanilla extract, cinnamon, remaining sugar, and the candied citron, if using. Moisten the ingredients with the plum brandy and stir well. Set aside to rest in a cool place for a day.

Gather three-quarters of the flour into a mound on a clean work surface and make a well in the center.

Dissolve the yeast in the warm milk and add to the well with 1 teaspoon of the sugar, the egg and yolk, and a pinch of salt. Mix, then knead to form a soft dough. Transfer to a bowl, cover, and leave to rise for about 1 hour. Add the remaining flour, butter, and sugar. Knead energetically and leave to proof for 30 minutes.

Grease an 8-inch/20-cm baking pan (tin) with a little butter and line with parchment paper. Roll out the dough into an 8 × 12-inch/20 × 30-cm rectangle. Spread the filling over the top, adding generous dollops of soft butter. Roll up the dough, seal the ends tightly, and stretch the resulting log to a length of 30 inches/75 cm. Gently wind the log into a coil, then tuck the loose end under the cake. Place in the pan, cover, and leave to rise until doubled in size.

Preheat the oven to 325 °F/160 °C/140 °C Fan/Gas 3. Brush the surface of the cake with the egg white and dust with sugar. Bake for about 1 hour, or until golden brown. Leave to cool before serving.

Emilia-Romagna

Salt and the wisdom of the food

Emilia-Romagna is the promised land for food-lovers. This rich epicurean region is home to a series of gourmet specialties that have even become synonymous with the Italian identity. We start with the wonderful gnocco fritto (page 128) and piadina (page 132) to accompany the delicious salumi and cheeses, followed by egg pasta, both filled and unfilled, such as the delectable lasagna of Bologna with its sumptuous ragù sauce (page 136); the marvelous tortellini of Castelfranco, which has always boasted an almost maternal bond with the surrounding countryside; and the humble passatelli, made with stale bread and cheese and cooked in a rich broth (page 134). On display in the region's gleaming delicatessens, known in Italy as *salumeria*— bastions of the gastronomic arts—are unique balsamic vinegars, Parma hams stamped with the five-pointed ducal crown, prized culatello di Zibello sausages cured by the mists of the Po, and of course the most famous Parmiggiano cheese, aged for a minimum of twelve months and up to forty-eight. You will also find the increasingly rare San Secondo shoulder ham, which was a particular favorite of Giuseppe Verdi, as well as pink mortadella from Bologna and the delightful zampone sausages from Modena (page 139). All of this is to be enjoyed with the sparkling Lambrusco wine made from grapes grown in vineyards in and around Modena.

Fried dough parcels

A mouthwatering delicacy, these puffy, golden, hollow pastries are made from a simple dough of flour and sparkling water and shared around the table accompanied by olives, cured meats, and cheese.

PREPARATION TIME 20 minutes
COOKING TIME 40 minutes
RESTING TIME 30 minutes
SERVES 8

1 pound 2 ounces/generous 4 cups/500 g Italian "0" flour
8–8½ fl oz/1–generous 1 cup/250–260 ml sparkling mineral water
1 ounce/scant ¼ cup/30 g lard, plus extra for frying
½ teaspoon baking soda (bicarbonate of soda)
Salt
Olives, cured meats, and cheese, to serve

Place the flour, a little salt, the sparkling mineral water, lard, and baking soda (bicarbonate of soda) in a large bowl and mix, then knead to form a smooth and elastic dough. Wrap in plastic wrap (cling film) and leave to rest at room temperature for 30 minutes.

Using a rolling pin, roll out the dough on a pastry board to a thickness of about ⅛ inch/4–5 mm. Using a fluted pastry wheel, cut out a large number of rectangles or diamond shapes.

Heat plenty of lard in a large skillet (frying pan) and fry the pastries in batches, turning them from side to side until they are fully puffed up and golden. Using a slotted spoon, remove them from the pan and drain on paper towels. Serve piping hot with olives, cured meats, and cheese.

Chard and cheese pie

Erbazzone

A savory pie also known as *scarpazzone*, typical of the Reggio Emilia province, and made using simple ingredients such as flour and lard for the pastry and vegetables from the garden for the filling.

PREPARATION TIME 30 minutes
COOKING TIME 50 minutes
RESTING TIME 45 minutes
SERVES 6–8

FOR THE PASTA MATTA (SIMPLE PIE DOUGH)
7 ounces/1⅔ cups/200 g Italian "00" flour
1 tablespoon lard, plus extra, melted, for brushing
2 tablespoons extra-virgin olive oil
3½ fl oz/scant ½ cup/100 ml lukewarm water
Salt

FOR THE FILLING
3 pounds/1.5 kg Swiss chard, washed well and fibrous parts
    of the ribs trimmed
2¼ ounces/60 g lardo (cured pork back fat), chopped
3 scallions (spring onions), sliced
1 clove garlic, chopped
4–5 handfuls grated Parmesan cheese
1 bunch parsley, coarsely chopped
Olive oil, for greasing
Black pepper

For the dough, put the flour and a pinch of salt into a large bowl and add the lard. Start mixing with a fork, then add the oil and continue working the dough. Add the water and knead by hand until the dough is smooth and elastic. Gather it into a ball, wrap it in plastic wrap (cling film), and leave to rest in the refrigerator for at least 45 minutes. Alternatively, you can use a stand mixer to make the dough.

Meanwhile, prepare the filling. Wash the chard very carefully to remove any remaining soil. Cook the chard in a large saucepan of boiling salted water for 5 minutes. Drain and set aside to cool, before squeezing out as much of the liquid as possible. Cut it into large chunks. Set aside.

Fry the lardo in a skillet (frying pan) to release the fat. Add the scallions (spring onions) and garlic to flavor the fat and sauté for 5 minutes. Add the chard and cook until wilted. Transfer to a bowl and add the grated

Parmesan and parsley. Season with salt and pepper and set aside.

Preheat the oven to 400 °F/200 °C/180 °C Fan/Gas 6. Lightly grease a 10-inch/25-cm square baking pan (tin).

Divide the chilled dough into several portions and, using a rolling pin or pasta machine, roll it out into thin sheets, about 12 inches/30 cm long. Line the prepared baking pan with some of the pastry sheets, allowing the excess to hang over the sides. Add the filling, then cover with the remaining sheets and create characteristic wrinkles on the top. Fold the overhanging edges inward, prick all over the surface of the pastry with a fork, and brush it with a little melted lard.

Bake in the preheated oven for 30 minutes, or until the top is golden brown. Remove from the oven and set aside to cool before cutting it into squares and serving.

Romagna-style piadina

Piadina Romagnola is an icon of Romagna cuisine, so much so that it has been granted PGI status. The specific rules apply to the making of the flatbread, but the fillings are up to you!

PREPARATION TIME 15 minutes
COOKING TIME 30 minutes
RESTING TIME 1 hour
MAKES 8–9

1 pound 2 ounces/generous 4 cups/500 g soft wheat flour, plus
   extra for dusting
¼ ounce/8 g baking powder
¼ ounce/2 teaspoons/10 g salt
1 tablespoon lard, at room temperature
Prosciutto, to serve
Squacquerone cheese, to serve
Arugula (rocket), to serve

Put the flour, 8 fl oz/1 cup/250 ml water, the baking powder, salt, and lard into the bowl of a stand mixer fitted with a dough hook and mix until it forms a dough. Transfer the dough to a clean work surface and knead briefly with your hands until it becomes very smooth. Gather the dough into a ball, wrap it in plastic wrap (cling film), and leave it to rest at room temperature for 1 hour.

Divide the dough into 3–3½ ounce/80–100 g portions, depending on the size of the skillet (frying pan) to be used for cooking them. Using a rolling pin, roll out the dough on a lightly floured work surface (or covered with parchment paper) into ¹⁄₁₆–⅛-inch/2–3-mm thick disks.

Heat a nonstick skillet over medium heat, then cook one piadina at a time, turning it constantly with one hand so that it cooks evenly. Each piadina should cook for 2 minutes on each side and is ready when it has turned a light golden color and developed the characteristic *macò*, or small dark spots, on the surface.

While still hot, transfer the piadina to a chopping board and cut it in half with a knife. Fill some of the flatbreads with prosciutto and others with Squacquerone cheese and arugula (rocket) and serve.

Passatelli soup

Passatelli are dumplings resembling short, fat spaghetti, created using a passatelli press or potato ricer. Traditionally flavored with nutmeg and lemon, and cooked for a few minutes in a meat broth (stock).

PREPARATION TIME 20 minutes

COOKING TIME 10 minutes

RESTING TIME 2 hours

SERVES 4

3½ ounces/2 cups/100 g fine bread crumbs, plus extra as needed

3½ ounces/1¼ cups/100 g grated Parmesan cheese, plus extra as needed

2 eggs (about 3½ ounces/100 g)

Grated nutmeg

Grated zest of 1 lemon

About 50 fl oz/6 cups/1.5 liters meat broth (stock)

All-purpose (plain) flour, for dusting (optional)

Salt and black pepper

Place the bread crumbs and grated cheese in a large bowl. Beat the eggs in a second bowl and season with salt, pepper, lemon zest, and nutmeg, to taste. Using a fork, start to combine the two mixtures until a dough forms. Knead the dough into a smooth and soft ball. If it's too firm, dilute it with a little of the meat broth (stock); if it's too wet, add more bread crumbs and cheese. Cover the dough in plastic wrap (cling film) and leave to rest at room temperature for 2 hours.

Bring the meat broth to a boil in a large saucepan.

Divide the dough in half and firmly press each half through a potato ricer with large holes. The resulting passatelli should be about 1½ inches/4 cm long. Alternatively, you can use a typical passatelli press. Take a portion of dough, roll it out on a floured pastry board until it is about ¾ inch/ 2 cm thick, and place the press on top. Apply pressure while slowly sliding forward so that the formed dumplings come out of the holes.

Add the dumplings to the stock and cook for 2 minutes, or until they float to the top. Serve the piping-hot soup and dumplings immediately.

Tortellini soup

These mini stuffed egg pasta pockets are said to resemble the navel of the goddess Venus. The traditional filling includes prosciutto, mortadella, pork loin, and Parmesan.

PREPARATION TIME 2 hours 30 minutes

COOKING TIME 15 minutes

RESTING TIME 2–14 hours

SERVES 4–6

14 ounces/3⅓ cups/400 g Italian "00" flour, plus extra for dusting
4 eggs
About 50 fl oz/6 cups/1.5 liters meat or capon broth (stock)

FOR THE FILLING
¾ ounce/1½ tablespoons/20 g unsalted butter
5½ ounces/150 g pork loin, sliced and cut into cubes
3½ ounces/100 g prosciutto
5½ ounces/150 g mortadella, sliced
5½ ounces/generous 1¾ cups/150 g grated Parmesan cheese
1 egg
Grated nutmeg, to taste
Salt and black pepper

For the filling, melt the butter in a nonstick skillet (frying pan), add the pork loin, and brown it on all sides. Remove from the pan and set aside to cool, then transfer it to a food processor together with the prosciutto, sliced mortadella, grated cheese, egg, and nutmeg. Finely chop the ingredients in short pulses until well combined. Only adjust the seasoning with salt and pepper at the end, bearing in mind that it will subsequently be wrapped in pasta. Cover the filling with plastic wrap (cling film) and leave it to rest in the refrigerator for at least 1 hour, or preferably overnight to allow the ingredients to absorb the flavors.

The next day, make the pasta. Gather the flour into a mound on a clean work surface and make a well in the center. Add the eggs to the well and mix and knead to a smooth and elastic dough. Place it in a food storage bag and leave to rest at room temperature for 1 hour.

Dust two large baking sheets with flour or line with parchment paper. Using a rolling pin or pasta machine, roll out the pasta into a thin sheet, then using a pastry cutter, cut out 1¼-inch/3–3.5-cm squares and place a little filling in the center. Immediately cover the pasta that is not being used to prevent it from drying out too much. To form the tortellini, fold each square in half to form a triangle. Press around the filling with your fingers to release the air, then seal the pasta. Make a ring by bringing together the two lower corners around your finger. Overlap the dough a little and pinch to seal. Arrange the finished tortellini on the prepared baking sheets and continue until all the pasta and filling are used up.

Bring the meat or capon broth to a boil in a large saucepan. Add the tortellini and cook until al dente, 1–2 minutes, then remove with a ladle to serving bowls. Serve the tortellini and broth piping hot.

Lasagna

The famous rich and tasty pasta of Bologna, with layers of egg and spinach pasta, creamy béchamel sauce, and a classic meat sauce (ragú), this is a dish to share with family and friends.

PREPARATION TIME 1 hour 30 minutes

COOKING TIME 3 hours

RESTING TIME 1 hour

SERVES 4–6

14 ounces/400 g spinach

12 ounces/3 cups/350 g Italian "00" flour, plus extra for dusting

3 eggs

1½ batches béchamel sauce (page 168)

Grated Parmesan cheese, for sprinkling

FOR THE BOLOGNESE SAUCE

2 tablespoons olive oil

3¼ ounces/¾ stick/90 g unsalted butter

1 onion, 1 celery stalk, and 1 carrot, chopped

5 ounces/150 g flat pancetta, chopped

1 pound 9 ounces/scant 6 cups/700 g ground (minced) beef and pork (pork loin and chuck steak)

1¾ fl oz/scant ¼ cup/50 ml dry white wine

17 fl oz/2 cups/500 ml puréed strained tomatoes (passata)

2 tablespoons tomato paste (purée)

Salt and black pepper

For the bolognese sauce, heat the oil and butter in a pan, add the onion, and sauté until lightly colored, then add the celery and carrot and sauté until colored too. Add the pancetta and cook for 1 minute, then add the ground (minced) meat. Sauté over a high heat, stirring continuously and breaking up the clumps with a wooden spoon. Once browned, season with salt and pepper. Pour the wine into the pan and stir to deglaze, then allow the wine to evaporate. Stir in the puréed strained tomatoes (passata) and the tomato paste (purée). Bring to a boil, cover with a lid and gently simmer for 2 hours.

Meanwhile, put the spinach into a pan with about ¾ inch/2 cm water, season with salt, partly cover with a lid, and cook until wilted. Drain the spinach, refresh under cold running water, and squeeze to remove as much water as possible. Chop the spinach finely.

To make the pasta sheets, gather the flour into a mound on a work surface and make a well in the center. Add the eggs and spinach to the well, and mix, then knead to a smooth and elastic dough. Alternatively, use a stand mixer fitted with a dough hook. Wrap the dough

in plastic wrap (cling film) and leave to rest at room temperature for at least 1 hour.

Roll out the dough on a floured pastry board to a relatively thin sheet and cut out rectangles slightly smaller than your baking pan (tin). Bring a saucepan of water to a boil. Add salt and a little oil and boil one pasta rectangle at a time, turning it over. When it rises to the surface, transfer it with a slotted spoon to a bowl of cold water, then drain and pat it dry with a cloth.

Preheat the oven to 400 °F/200 °C/180 °C Fan/Gas 6. Lay the first pasta sheet inside the baking pan. Add a layer of béchamel sauce, then a layer of meat sauce. Sprinkle with plenty of grated cheese. Add another pasta sheet and repeat until all the ingredients are used up. Finish with a last pasta sheet and a sprinkling of cheese. Before baking, cut the lasagna into portions with a knife, then bake for about 45 minutes, or until piping hot throughout. If it starts to brown too much, cover it with aluminum foil. Turn the broiler on, then broil the lasagna for a few minutes. Remove from the oven, leave for 5 minutes, then serve.

Pig's trotter with lentils

Zampone con lenticchie

Zampone di Modena (PGI)—stuffed pig's trotter—is a specialty of the region; this dish is traditionally served on New Year's Eve as the lentils are believed to bring luck for the year ahead.

PREPARATION TIME 30 minutes

COOKING TIME 2 hours 30 minutes

SOAKING TIME 3 hours

SERVES 4

9 ounces/scant 1½ cups/250 g dried brown lentils
1 (2-pound/4-ounce/1-kg) zampone (stuffed pig's foot/trotter)
2 tablespoons olive oil
1 tablespoon unsalted butter
1 fresh sage leaf, chopped
1 ounce/30 g pancetta, chopped
1 carrot, chopped
1 celery stalk, chopped
1 onion, chopped
1 pound 2 ounces/500 g tomatoes, chopped
Salt and black pepper

Soak the lentils in a large bowl of water for 3 hours. Using a slotted spoon, remove any that float to the surface, then drain the remainder and cook them in a large saucepan of boiling lightly salted water for 1 hour 30 minutes, or until tender.

Prepare and cook the zampone according to the packet instructions.

Heat the oil and butter in another large saucepan. Add the sage, pancetta, carrot, celery, and onion and sauté for 10 minutes, stirring frequently. Add the tomatoes, season with salt and pepper, and cook for at least 15 minutes. Drain the lentils and stir them into the tomatoes. Allow them to absorb the flavor for 10 minutes.

Remove the pan with the pig's trotter from the heat and leave it to stand in its cooking water for 10 minutes. Drain and cut the zampone into slices, arrange them in a serving dish, and spread the stewed lentils around. Serve piping hot.

Carnival fritters

Typical of the Romagna region, castagnole are deep-fried dough balls flavored with grappa, lemon, and vanilla, and traditionally served as a sweet treat during Carnival.

PREPARATION TIME 30 minutes

COOKING TIME 20 minutes

SERVES 8

1 ounce/¼ stick/30 g unsalted butter, softened

3 tablespoons superfine (caster) sugar

1 tablespoon plus 1½ teaspoons grappa

Grated zest of 1 lemon

½ vanilla bean (pod), split lengthwise and seeds scraped out

2 eggs

9 ounces/2 cups/250 g all-purpose (plain) flour, plus extra for dusting

¼ ounce/8 g baking powder

Vegetable oil, for deep-frying

Confectioners' (icing) sugar, for dusting

Put the butter, superfine (caster) sugar, grappa, grated lemon zest, and the vanilla seeds into a large bowl. Add an egg and about one-third of the flour and stir to combine (the butter will not melt completely, but this is fine at this stage). Stir in the baking powder, then add the remaining egg.

Add another third of the flour and mix. Transfer the dough to a pastry board and add the remaining flour.

Knead the dough until it is smooth, soft, and no longer sticky. Take portions of the dough and knead them briefly with your hands to form cylinders with a diameter of about ¾ inch/2 cm.

Using a knife, cut each dough cylinder into small chunks, then roll them into hazelnut-size balls. As you make them, set them aside on one side of the flour-dusted pastry board.

Heat enough oil for deep-frying in a large, deep saucepan to 350 °F/180 °C on a thermometer, or until a cube of bread browns in 30 seconds. Add a few dough balls at a time and deep-fry, turning them several times, until they are puffy and golden brown. Using a slotted spoon, remove them from the oil and drain on paper towels. Dust with confectioners' (icing sugar) according to preference and serve.

140

Modena-style chocolate and coffee cake

This crumbly, flourless chocolate and coffee cake from Modena was created at the Pasticceria Gollini in nearby Vignola. The original recipe remains a secret, but this is a very close interpretation.

PREPARATION TIME 30 minutes

COOKING TIME 40 minutes

SERVES 6

3 ounces/¾ stick/80 g unsalted butter, cut into small pieces, plus extra for greasing

All-purpose (plain) flour, for dusting

9 ounces/250 g dark chocolate, broken into pieces

4 eggs, separated

5½ ounces/⅔ cup/150 g superfine (caster) sugar

1 teaspoon lemon juice

3½ ounces/¾ cup/100 g blanched almonds, finely chopped

3 tablespoons instant coffee granules

1 shot glass rum, about ¾ fl oz/4 teaspoons/25ml

Preheat the oven to 350 °F/180 °C/160 °C Fan/Gas 4. Grease a 2-pound/900-g loaf pan (tin) with butter and add a dusting of flour.

Place the chocolate in a heatproof bowl and set over a saucepan of gently simmering water, making sure the bottom of the bowl doesn't touch the water, and leave to melt. Remove from the heat and mix in the butter.

Whisk the egg yolks and sugar together in a large bowl with an electric whisk until pale and frothy. Whisk the egg whites and lemon juice in a separate bowl until stiff peaks form.

Add the chopped almonds, melted chocolate, coffee, rum, and the whisked egg whites to the egg yolk mixture and gently fold in until combined.

Pour the mixture into the prepared loaf pan, cover with parchment paper, and bake in the preheated oven for 30 minutes. Turn out the cake and leave it to cool before serving.

Tuscany 147

Center

Marche 163

Umbria 175

Lazio 189

Tuscany

The inalienable pleasure of meat

To have a taste of Tuscany almost always means ordering a superb steak, or as the locals say, a *fiorentina*. And it has to be Chianina. Real Chianina steak, from the Chiana Valley, comes from a wonderful cow that is exclusively reared for its tender and flavorful meat. To have a taste of Tuscany also means discovering Italy's finest oils, strong-flavored like those from Chianti, or pale and delicate like those from Lucca. It means discovering flavors that are sometimes quite strong, like that of game, such as the wild boar to be found in the forests of the Maremma region; or of the unrivaled pecorino cheeses made in Crete Senesi and Casentino; like that of the gloriously velvety zolfino beans that can be found in jars, cooked according to an ancient recipe; or of delicate, tender, and aromatic lardo di Colonnata. The region's cuisine has also made good use of the bountiful fish and seafood from the coast, resulting in such historical dishes as cacciucco alla Livornese (page 155). Then there are grains, legumes (pulses), and vegetables used in the traditional soups such as ribollita (page 152), pancotti, and pappe col pomodoro, kept warm in a rustic terracotta pot known as a *coccio*. The region also has a strong tradition of sweet treats, both dry and soft, including cantucci (page 159) and zuccotti, castagnacci (page 160) and panforti. The bounty of Tuscany is also found in its wines, from the celebrated, award-winning Brunello di Montalcino to Chianti Classico.

Anchovy and liver crostini

Crostini neri all'aretina

The word "crostini" refers to a bite-sized piece of bread with a topping—similar to bruschetta, but smaller! Toppings can vary from the simple to the more elaborate, as here.

PREPARATION TIME 15 minutes

COOKING TIME 20–25 minutes

SERVES 8

2 ounces/3½ tablespoons/50 g butter

3 tablespoons olive oil

1 white onion, thinly sliced

2 tablespoons chopped parsley, plus extra to garnish

10½ ounces/300 g chicken livers, trimmed

5 tablespoons Vin Santo or other white wine

6 fl oz/¾ cup/175 ml beef stock

9 ounces/250 g calf's spleen or liver, chopped

1–2 oil-packed anchovy fillets, drained and chopped

1 tablespoon capers, drained, rinsed, and chopped

16 thin slices Tuscan bread, toasted

Salt and black pepper

Melt half the butter with the oil in a skillet (frying pan). Add the onion, parsley, and chicken livers and cook for a few minutes over a medium-high heat, stirring frequently, for 5 minutes. Reduce the heat to medium-low and cook, stirring frequently, for another 10 minutes. Pour in the wine and cook, stirring, for a few minutes until the alcohol has evaporated, then season with pepper and remove the pan from the heat.

Turn the mixture out onto a chopping board and chop with a mezzaluna or a heavy kitchen knife. Transfer the mixture to a shallow pan and add the remaining butter, the stock, and calf's spleen or liver. Cook over a low heat, stirring occasionally, for a few minutes, but do not let the mixture dry out. Remove the pan from the heat, add the anchovies and capers, season lightly with salt, and mix well. Briefly dip one side of each slice of toast into the hot stock and spoon some of the liver mixture on top. Sprinkle with parsley and serve.

Tomato and caper crostini

Crostini rossi alla chiantigiana

Tomatoes are the star in this "red" crostini topping, typical of Chianti, in the heart of Tuscany. A selection of different crostini is the perfect antipasto to start your Tuscan feast.

PREPARATION TIME 25 minutes

SERVES 4

7 ounces/200 g whole wheat (wholemeal) bread

4 tablespoons white wine vinegar

2 large ripe tomatoes, skinned, seeded, and chopped

1 tablespoon capers, drained, rinsed, and chopped

3 tablespoons chopped flat-leaf parsley

2 tablespoons chopped thyme

1 clove garlic, chopped

3 tablespoons olive oil

8 thin slices Tuscan bread, toasted, or pan-fried polenta

Salt and black pepper

Tear the whole wheat (wholemeal) bread into pieces and put them into a medium bowl. Pour in the vinegar and leave to soak for 5 minutes, then drain and squeeze well. Transfer to a mortar or another bowl, add the tomatoes, capers, parsley, thyme, garlic, and oil, and season with salt and pepper. Pound with a pestle or the end of a rolling pin to form a coarse mixture. Spread the mixture on slices of toasted bread or pan-fried polenta and serve.

Sage fritters

Salvia—sage—grows in abundance across the region and has been used in Tuscan cooking for centuries, in stews, pasta dishes, or simply deep-fried in batter, as here, for the perfect appetizer.

PREPARATION TIME 25 minutes

COOKING TIME 15 minutes

SERVES 5

3½ ounces/generous ¾ cup/100 g all-purpose (plain) flour
1 egg
Anchovy paste, for spreading
20 large fresh sage leaves
Vegetable oil, for deep-frying
Salt

Sift the flour with a pinch of salt into a large bowl and make a well in the center. Add the egg to the well and beat, incorporating the flour gradually with a balloon whisk or wooden spoon. Gradually whisk in 7 fl oz/scant 1 cup/200 ml ice water until smooth.

Spread a little anchovy paste on one side of each sage leaf and sandwich them together in pairs.

Heat enough oil for deep-frying in a large, deep saucepan to 350–375 °F/180–190 °C on a thermometer, or until a cube of bread browns in 30 seconds. Using tongs, dip the sage leaves into the batter, shake off the excess, and add to the hot oil in batches. Deep-fry for a few minutes until light golden brown. Remove with a slotted spoon, drain on paper towels, and serve hot.

Spinach and ricotta dumplings

Gnudi—"nude ravioli"—is particularly popular in the south of Tuscany, in Siena and Grosseto. These little dumplings are traditionally made from spinach and ricotta and served in a butter and sage sauce.

PREPARATION TIME 25 minutes

COOKING TIME 10 minutes

SERVES 4

1 pound 2 ounces/500 g spinach, coarse stalks removed

1 pound/¾ cup/450 g ricotta cheese

3½ ounces/generous ¾ cup/100 g grated pecorino cheese, plus extra for serving

2 eggs, lightly beaten

Grated nutmeg

3½ ounces/generous ¾ cup/100 g plain (all-purpose) flour, plus extra for dusting

2 ounces/3½ tablespoons/50 g butter

10–12 fresh sage leaves

Salt and black pepper

Wash the spinach in cold running water, then place in a large pan with the water still clinging to the leaves. Cook over low heat, turning once or twice, for about 5 minutes, until wilted. Drain well, squeezing out as much liquid as possible, and chop very finely. Tip into a bowl and stir in the ricotta, pecorino cheese, and eggs. Add a little grated nutmeg and season with salt and pepper.

Bring a large pan of salted water to a boil. Using a teaspoon, shape small rounded dumplings from the spinach and ricotta mixture, dust with flour, and add to the pan. Cook for 1–2 minutes until they float to the top. Remove with a slotted spoon and transfer to a warmed serving dish.

Tuscan vegetable soup

A classic Tuscan soup of humble origins—made with beans, vegetables, and day-old bread. Some variations across the region see ham and bacon rind added to the dish for a nonvegetarian version.

PREPARATION TIME 30 minutes

COOKING TIME 2 hours 40 minutes

SOAKING TIME 12 hours

SERVES 4–6

1 pound 2 ounces/2¾ cups/500 g dried cannellini beans

3 tablespoons olive oil

1 onion, coarsely chopped

1 celery stalk, coarsely chopped

2–3 carrots, coarsely chopped

2 potatoes, diced

1–2 zucchini (courgettes), sliced

1 bunch Swiss chard leaves, shredded

1 savoy or summer cabbage, or 1 bunch Tuscan kale (cavolo nero), shredded

1 sprig flat-leaf parsley, finely chopped

1 day-old rustic loaf, very thinly sliced

Salt and black pepper

Soak the cannellini beans in a large bowl of water overnight. The next day, drain and put them into a large saucepan, cover with water, and bring to a boil. Reduce the heat and simmer for 40 minutes.

Meanwhile, heat the oil in another large saucepan. Add the onion, celery, carrots, potatoes, and zucchini (courgettes) and cook over a very low heat, stirring occasionally, for 30 minutes. Season with salt, add the Swiss chard and cabbage, and cook, stirring, for a few minutes. Cover the pan with a lid.

Drain the beans, setting aside the cooking liquid. Press half the beans through a fine-mesh strainer (sieve) into a bowl, then stir the purée into the pan of vegetables. Add the reserved cooking liquid and simmer for 1 hour. Add the remaining whole beans and parsley and simmer for another 1–1½ hours.

Remove the soup from the heat and season with salt and pepper to taste. Make a layer of bread slices in a tureen and ladle some of the soup over it. Continue making alternate layers of bread and soup until all the ingredients have been used, then let stand until the bread is completely soaked. Serve immediately.

Livornese-style
fish soup

A bold and hearty fish soup emblematic of Livorno, always served with toasted garlic-rubbed bread and red wine. The dish should include at least four different varieties of seafood.

PREPARATION TIME 1 hour

COOKING TIME 1 hour

SERVES 6

9¼ fl oz/generous 1 cup/275 ml olive oil

5 garlic cloves, peeled and left whole

6 fresh sage leaves

1 dried red chile

1 pound 12 ounces/800 g cleaned octopus, cut into pieces

1 pound 9 ounces/700 g cleaned mixed squid and cuttlefish, halved if large

1 pound/450 g huss or shark fillet, thickly sliced

9¼ fl oz/generous 1 cup/275 ml red wine

2 tablespoons plus 1½ teaspoons tomato paste (purée)

1 celery stalk, chopped

10½ ounces/300 g scorpion fish, cleaned and cut into chunks

1 pound 9 ounces/700 g tomatoes, skinned, seeded, and diced

1 pound/450 g large and medium raw shrimp (prawns), peeled and deveined

12 slices Tuscan bread

Heat half the oil in a large, shallow pan. Add three of the garlic cloves, the sage, and chile and cook, stirring frequently, for a few minutes, or until the garlic is golden. Remove the aromatics with a slotted spoon and discard them.

Add the octopus and mixed squid and cuttlefish and cook for 3 minutes, then add the huss or shark and cook for another 3 minutes. Pour in the wine. Mix the tomato paste (purée) with 6 fl oz/¾ cup/175 ml water in a small bowl, then stir into the pan. Simmer gently for 30 minutes.

Heat the remaining oil in a medium pan. Meanwhile, chop one of the remaining garlic cloves. Add the celery and chopped garlic to the pan and cook over a low heat, stirring occasionally, for 5 minutes. Add the scorpion

fish and tomatoes, pour in 3–4 tablespoons water, and simmer gently for 20 minutes.

Transfer the contents of the smaller pan into the larger pan and check to make sure the seafood is cooked. Add the shrimp (prawns) and cook for 2–3 minutes, then remove the pan from the heat.

Toast the slices of bread on both sides, rub them with the remaining garlic clove, and put them all around the edge of a warmed serving dish. Ladle the stew into the center and serve immediately. You could also put the bread into six individual bowls, ladle the stew on top, and serve.

Florentine-style steak

The Florentines simply call this *bistecca*—derived from
the English word "beefsteak"—and it is a dish that is
truly symbolic of the region, made with a porterhouse
or T-bone steak.

PREPARATION TIME 5 minutes

COOKING TIME 10 minutes

SERVES 4

1 × 2 pound 10-ounce/1.2-kg porterhouse or T-bone steak
Olive oil, for drizzling
Salt and black pepper

Preheat the broiler (grill). Add the steak and broil (grill) for
5 minutes on each side, or until browned on the outside
and just pink inside. Remove from the heat and sprinkle
with salt. Drizzle a ring of oil in a warmed serving dish,
lay the steak on top, and serve immediately, sprinkled
with pepper.

Cantucci

Birthplace of the cantucci, the Antonio Mattei bakery in Prato still produces these traditional almond-flavored cookies (biscuits) using their original recipe from 1858.

PREPARATION TIME 30 minutes

COOKING TIME 40 minutes

SERVES 4

Butter, for greasing

1 pound 2 ounces/generous 4 cups/500 g self-rising (self-raising) flour, plus extra for dusting

1 pound 2 ounces/scant 2¼ cups/500 g superfine (caster) sugar

1 teaspoon baking powder

3 eggs

2 egg yolks

Pinch of saffron threads, crushed

9 ounces/2 cups/250 g shelled almonds, in their skins

Salt

Preheat the oven to 325 °F/160 °C/140 °C Fan/Gas 3. Grease two large baking sheets with butter and dust with flour.

Sift the flour, sugar, baking powder, and a pinch of salt into a mound on a clean work surface and make a well in the center. Break two eggs into the well and add the egg yolks and saffron. Gradually incorporate the dry ingredients with your fingers, then add the almonds and mix well.

Using floured hands, take small pieces of the dough and shape into long rolls, about 1¼–1¾ inches/2–3 cm wide and ½ inch/1 cm thick. Put the rolls onto the prepared baking sheets. Lightly beat the remaining egg in a small bowl and brush the tops of the cookies. Bake in the preheated oven for 30 minutes.

Remove from the oven and cut into 1¼–1½-inch/3–4-cm pieces at an angle, then return to the oven and cook for 5 minutes each side until golden brown. When completely cool, store in an airtight container.

Pistoian-style chestnut cake

This recipe should be made with the freshest chestnut flour—it's best to keep this flour in the refrigerator. If you can find it, use flour from Monte Amiata, where chestnuts are cultivated and grow in abundance.

PREPARATION TIME 20 minutes

COOKING TIME 40 minutes

SOAKING TIME 15 minutes

SERVES 6–8

2 ounces/⅓ cup/50 g raisins
3 tablespoons olive oil, plus extra for brushing
1 pound 5 ounces/5 cups/600 g very fresh chestnut flour
1 teaspoon salt
3½ ounces/¾ cup/100 g pine nuts
3½ ounces/¾ cup/100 g shelled walnuts, coarsely chopped
1 small sprig rosemary

Place the raisins in a small bowl, pour in warm water to cover, and soak for 15 minutes, or until plumped up. Drain, squeeze out the excess water, and pat dry with paper towels.

Preheat the oven to 425 °F/220 °C/200 °C Fan/Gas 7. Brush a 12-inch/30-cm round cake pan (tin) with about 3 tablespoons oil.

Sift the chestnut flour into a large bowl and gradually stir in about 30 fl oz/3¾ cups/900 ml water to make a smooth batter. Stir in the salt, pine nuts, and raisins and mix well. Pour the mixture into the prepared pan and sprinkle with the walnuts and a few rosemary needles.

Drizzle with the oil, place the pan on a baking sheet, and bake in the preheated oven for 40 minutes, or until the top is golden and the surface is cracked. Remove from the oven and leave to cool slightly, then serve.

Marche

The many merits of pigs and fish

The Marche region, whose landscapes retain the charm of yesteryear, is where nature seems to be at its best. In fact, all along the coast, from Gabicce to Porto d'Ascoli, her bounty is evident in the sea, with nets straining with all kinds of fish; while inland, she has hidden white truffles in the Acqualagna area and black truffles almost everywhere. In the Piceno region, she hangs small and tender Ascolane olives on the trees, and sees cows, sheep, and pigs in the meadows and countryside. Interpreting these gifts in the best possible way has led to an incredible variety of soups, broths, and grilled meats. Olives are first stuffed with a creamy meat filling and then browned and fried (page 164); handmade piconi are flavored with cheese and chocolate; cured meats abound, from the rare, such as the legendary ciaiuscolo di Macerata, a creamy pink sausage to spread on slices of homemade bread, to the mild Fabriano salami and prized prosciutto di Carpegna. There are also special cheeses, such as those from Talamello known as *formaggi di fossa*, "pit cheeses," which ripen in chambers dug under the streets, wrapped in white cloths, and the casciotta cheese produced in Urbino. True connoisseurs can pair all these delicacies with wines: with white Verdicchio dei Castelli di Jesi and Verdicchio di Matelica, or the reds Rosso Piceno and Rosso Conero.

Ascoli-style stuffed olives

A traditional antipasto from the Marche region, these deep-fried, meat-stuffed green olives are found all over Italy. Named for the town of Ascoli Piceno, the original recipe is believed to date from the nineteenth century.

PREPARATION TIME 20 minutes

COOKING TIME 20 minutes

MAKES 30

2 tablespoons extra-virgin olive oil

½ onion, chopped

1 carrot, chopped

1 celery stalk, chopped

2 ounces/scant ½ cup/50 g ground (minced) lean beef

2 ounces/scant ½ cup/50 g ground (minced) lean pork

2 ounces/scant ½ cup/50 g ground (minced) chicken

1¾ fl oz/scant ¼ cup/50 ml white wine

30 large green olives, rinsed and pitted

Pinch of ground nutmeg

Grated zest of 1 lemon

2 ounces/50 g grated Parmesan cheese

2 eggs

Italian "00" flour, for coating

Bread crumbs, for coating

Vegetable oil, for deep-frying

Salt and black pepper

Heat the olive oil in a large skillet (frying pan), add the onion, carrot, and celery, and sauté for a few minutes. Add all the meat and cook slowly over a low heat, pouring in the wine and stirring to scrape up all the crispy bits from the bottom of the pan. Season with salt and pepper.

Meanwhile, use a paring knife to cut a spiral through the olives from the top to the base. Set aside.

When the meat is cooked and warm, transfer it to a blender, adding the nutmeg, lemon zest, cheese, and 1 egg, and blend. Using wet hands, shape the mixture into hazelnut-size balls. Reform the olives by wrapping them around the balls of filling.

For the coating, spread some flour out on a large plate. Lightly beat the remaining egg and add to a shallow dish, then spread the bread crumbs out on another large plate. Roll the olives in the flour until coated, then dip them into the egg, then roll them in the bread crumbs until coated all over.

Heat enough oil for deep-frying in a large, deep saucepan to 350 °F/180 °C, or until a cube of bread browns in 30 seconds. Carefully add the olives to the hot oil in batches and deep-fry until crispy. Remove with a slotted spoon and leave to drain on paper towels.

Serve the stuffed olives while still hot.

Rum and chocolate half-moons

Another specialty from Ascoli Piceno, these sweet baked ravioli-style parcels are filled with ricotta, chocolate, and rum. There is also a savory version made with pecorino cheese and served at Easter.

PREPARATION TIME 45 minutes

COOKING TIME 15 minutes

CHILLING TIME 15 minutes

SERVES 6

FOR THE PIE CRUST (SHORTCRUST PASTRY)
1 pound 2 ounces/generous 4 cups/500 g all-purpose (plain) flour, plus extra for dusting

7 ounces/generous ¾ cup/200 g superfine (caster) sugar

9 ounces/2¼ sticks/250 g unsalted butter, softened

4 egg yolks

FOR THE FILLING
1 pound 2 ounces/scant 2¼ cups/500 g ewe's milk ricotta cheese

3 egg yolks

5 ounces/1½ cups/150 g confectioners' (icing) sugar

Pinch of ground cinnamon

Grated zest of 2 lemons

1¾ fl oz/scant ¼ cup/50 ml rum

3½ ounces/100 g dark chocolate, grated

3 ounces/scant ⅔ cup/80 g shelled almonds, chopped

1 egg, for brushing

For the pie crust (shortcrust pastry), gather the flour into a mound on a clean work surface and make a well in the center. Add the sugar, butter, and egg yolks to the well and quickly mix everything together to make a soft and smooth dough. Transfer the dough to a bowl, cover with plastic wrap (cling film), and leave to rest in the refrigerator for 15 minutes.

Preheat the oven to 350 °F/180 °C/160 °C Fan/Gas 4. Line a large baking sheet with parchment paper.

For the filling, press the cheese through a fine-mesh strainer (sieve) into a large bowl. Add the egg yolks, sugar, cinnamon, grated lemon zest, rum, chocolate, and chopped almonds and mix until smooth.

Roll out the dough fairly thinly on a lightly floured work surface and cut out 2¾–3¼-inch/7–8-cm-diameter disks. Place a hazelnut-shaped mound of filling in the center of each disk and fold it into a crescent shape, pressing tightly along the edge with your fingers to seal.

Lay the filled half-moons pastries on the prepared baking sheet, brush them with beaten egg, prick them with a toothpick (cocktail stick), and bake in the preheated oven for 15 minutes. Remove from the oven and serve warm.

Wild mushroom and chicken baked pasta

An incredibly luxurious dish and a signature of the Marche region, vincisgrassi is similar to Emilia-Romagna's lasagna, but made from a richer mix of mushrooms, chicken livers, and sweetbreads.

PREPARATION TIME 1 hour

COOKING TIME 2 hours

INFUSING TIME 20 minutes

SERVES 6

12 ounces/scant 3 cups/350 g all-purpose (plain) flour, plus 2 ounces/scant ½ cup/50 g for the béchamel

7 ounces/scant 1½ cups/200 g semolina

3 eggs

1 ounce/¼ stick/30 g unsalted butter, melted, plus 2 ounces/½ stick/50 g butter for the béchamel

3 tablespoons Vin Santo or Marsala

3 ounces/1 cup/80 g grated cheese, to finish

17 fl oz/2 cups/500 ml whole (full-fat) milk

1 onion, halved, 1 bay leaf and a few cloves

Salt and black pepper

FOR THE MEAT SAUCE

1 ounce/30 g dried mushrooms, soaked in water until soft

3½ ounces/100 g sweetbreads

2 ounces/½ stick/30 g unsalted butter

2 tablespoons olive oil

½ onion, chopped

1 black truffle, brushed, washed, dried, and cut into small dice

Meat broth (stock), for moistening

1 boneless chicken breast, cut into strips

7 ounces/200 g chicken giblets

1¾ fl oz/scant 14 cup/50 ml dry Marsala

For the meat sauce, drain and chop the mushrooms. Cook the sweetbreads in simmering water for a few minutes, then drain, cool, and dice. Sauté the sweetbreads in half of the butter for a few minutes.

Heat the remaining butter and oil in a separate pan. Add the onion and sauté until translucent, then add the mushrooms, truffle and a little broth (stock). Add the chicken breast and sauté over high heat, then stir in the giblets and cook for a few minutes. Add the Marsala and allow to evaporate, then enough hot water to cover. Season, cover with a lid, and cook over low heat for 30 minutes. Add the sweetbreads off the heat.

For the pasta dough, gather the flour and semolina on a work surface and make a well in the center. Add the eggs, melted butter, a pinch of salt, and the Vin Santo. Mix and knead to form a smooth dough, then roll out and cut into 4 × 20-inch (10 × 50 cm) strips. Bring a pan of salted water to a boil. Add the dough strips and cook for 2–3 minutes. Drain and plunge them into a large bowl of cold water, then lay them on a damp cloth.

For the béchamel, bring the milk, onion, bay leaf, and cloves to a boil in a saucepan, then set aside to infuse for 20 minutes. Melt the butter in another pan, add the flour, and stir until a paste forms. Cook for another 2 minutes. Discard the aromatics, then gradually add the milk to the roux, stirring continuously. Cook for 5–10 minutes until the sauce thickens. Season to taste.

Preheat the oven to 350 °F/180 °C/160 °C Fan/Gas 4. Grease a large baking pan (tin) with butter. Arrange strips of dough in a crisscross pattern to cover the base of the pan with the excess hanging over the sides. Cut the remaining strips into rectangles. Alternate layers of dough with layers of meat sauce, grated cheese, and béchamel sauce, finishing with a layer of sauce. Use the overhanging strips to cover the pie. Cover with aluminum foil, place in a large roasting pan, and pour in enough water to come halfway up the sides. Bake for 40 minutes, then rest for 10 minutes before turning out.

St. Benedict's seafood stew

A stew originally created by the fishermen of San Benedetto del Tronto, the seafood is layered in the pot with the firmer specimens at the bottom; the essential ingredient of this specialty, however, is the vinegar.

PREPARATION TIME 1 hour

COOKING TIME 40 minutes

SERVES 8

10½ ounces/300 g mussels, cleaned (page 323)

10½ ounces/300 g clams, cleaned (page 323)

4–5 tablespoons olive oil

1 onion, finely chopped

10½ ounces/300 g small cuttlefish, skinned

1 green bell pepper, cored, seeded, and cut into large slices

5 underripe tomatoes, skinned, seeded, and chopped

1 dried chile, crumbled

3½ fl oz/scant ½ cup/100 ml white wine vinegar

5 pounds 8 ounces/2.5 kg assorted fish (e.g. scorpionfish, monkfish tail, red mullet), gutted and boned

10½ ounces/300 g mantis shrimp

Salt and black pepper

Place the mussels and clams in a large skillet (frying pan) over a high heat without any seasoning and cook until they open. Remove from the heat and discard any that remain closed.

Heat the oil in a large saucepan with a lid, add the onion, and sauté until it turns translucent. Add the skinned cuttlefish and cook for 10 minutes. Add the green bell pepper and season with salt and pepper. Stir and cook for 10 minutes over a low heat.

Add the tomatoes and chile, then pour in the vinegar and stir to scrape up all the crispy bits off the bottom of the pan, then allow it to evaporate.

Start layering the seafood, beginning with the less delicate fish and ending with the mussels, clams (half with shells and half without), and mantis shrimp. Cover with a lid and cook over a low heat for 20 minutes, adding hot water if necessary. Remove from the heat and serve.

Ancona-style cod

Stockfish—air-dried cod—is cooked slowly with potatoes, tomatoes, and a good-quality olive oil in this iconic dish from Ancona, the capital of the Marche region.

PREPARATION TIME 25 minutes

COOKING TIME 1 hour 50 minutes

SOAKING TIME 24 hours; RESTING TIME 20 minutes

SERVES 4–6

2 pounds 4 ounces/1 kg dried cod (stockfish)
3–3½ ounces/80–100 g salt-packed anchovy fillets
7 fl oz/scant 1 cup /200 ml extra-virgin olive oil, plus
    1 tablespoon for coating the pan
1 teaspoon white wine vinegar
½ onion, finely chopped
2 cloves garlic, finely chopped
2 ounces/1⅔ cups/50 g finely chopped parsley
1 small sprig rosemary, finely chopped
14 ounces/400 g ripe tomatoes, thinly sliced
2¼ ounces/½ cup/60 g pitted black olives
1 pound 2 ounces/500 g potatoes, cut into wedges
1¾ fl oz/scant ¼ cup/50 ml dry white wine
Salt and black pepper

Soak the stockfish in a large bowl of water in the refrigerator for at least 24 hours, changing the water several times. Drain and pat dry with paper towels. Cut it into medium-size pieces and set aside.

Soak the anchovies in a bowl of water for 5–20 minutes, then drain, remove any bones, finely chop, and set aside.

Add the 7 fl oz/scant 1 cup/200 ml olive oil and the vinegar to a large bowl and whisk to an emulsion. Season with a pinch of salt and pepper. Add the onion, garlic, parsley, rosemary, and anchovies and mix to combine.

Add the remaining 1 tablespoon of olive oil to a high-sided pan with a lid, swirling to coat, and cover the bottom of the pan with a layer of the stockfish. Drizzle

the fish with some of the flavored oil, then cover with half of the sliced tomatoes and olives. Season with salt and pepper. Make a second layer of stockfish pieces, drizzle with the flavored oil, and cover with the tomatoes and olives. Season with a pinch of salt and a sprinkling of pepper. Finish by covering everything with the potato wedges and drizzle with the flavored oil.

Place the pan over a high heat and when it comes to a simmer, pour in the wine. Stir to scrape up all the crispy bits off the bottom of the pan, then allow the alcohol to evaporate. Cover with the lid, reduce the heat to low, and cook for 1 hour 10 minutes. Uncover and finish cooking for another 30 minutes. Remove the pan from the heat and set aside to rest for about 20 minutes without stirring before serving.

Braised chicken

A dish served at Sunday lunch tables across the region, this soft braised chicken in a velvety sauce is traditionally flavored with garlic—which MUST be unpeeled!—rosemary, and white wine.

PREPARATION TIME 15 minutes

COOKING TIME 1 hour

SERVES 4

3 tablespoons extra-virgin olive oil

1 × 3 pound 8 ounce/1.6 kg whole chicken, skin-on,
   cut into medium pieces

1 clove garlic, unpeeled and left whole

3½ fl oz/scant ½ cup/100 ml dry white wine

1 small sprig rosemary

4–5 tablespoons puréed strained tomatoes (passata)

Salt and black pepper

Heat the oil in a Dutch oven or terracotta cooking pot, add the garlic clove, and sauté for a minute or two. Add the chicken pieces and brown well over a high heat until golden brown on all sides. Season with salt and pepper. Pour in the wine and allow the alcohol to evaporate.

Add the rosemary and puréed strained tomatoes (passata). Stir well, reduce the heat, cover with a lid, and braise for about 45 minutes. During this time, add a little hot water, if the pot becomes too dry. Toward the end, it might be a good idea to leave the lid ajar. The chicken should be well cooked and the sauce reduced.

Transfer to a serving dish and serve.

Umbria

Where spirit of the place nourishes both soul and palate

The mystical harmony of the landscape of Umbria predisposes the soul to enjoy the beautiful things in life. Naturally, food is one of them. Your eyes are soothed and enchanted by expanses of olive groves, making it possible to savor the different flavors of the oils produced in the Colli di Assisi and Spoleto, Colli Martani and Amerini, Colli Orvietani and Trasimeno, which combine wonderfully with the region's culinary delights, first and foremost the tiny and delicious Castelluccio lentils. Oil glistens on legumes (pulses), drips from the skewers of wood pigeons, sizzles in the pheasant casseroles (page 181), and in the fish stews for which expert hands bring together all the species to be found in Lake Trasimeno: eels and pike, perch and tench. On entering food shops, one immediately picks up an old-fashioned "larder smell," a mixture of the scents emanating from the cured hams, capocollo, salami, sausages—in short, from the *Norcineria*, a word derived from the small town of Norcia, the capital of pork processing. There is also an added earthy note of truffles. When climbing the hills of Torgiano and the heights of Montefalco, you are greeted by a sea of vineyards as far as the eye can see, building your anticipation to try the excellent red wines made from them.

Lentil and tomato soup

This tasty and nutritious starter dish is made with Castelluccio di Norcia lentils, which have PGI status. The small, thin-skinned lentils are perfect for soups that don't feature pasta or other grains.

PREPARATION TIME 15 minutes

COOKING TIME 40 minutes

SERVES 4

9 ounces/scant 1½ cups/250 g Castelluccio di Norcia lentils
1 slice lardo (cured pork back fat), finely chopped
½ clove garlic, chopped
2 tablespoons chopped parsley
4 medium ripe tomatoes, diced
2–3 fresh sage leaves
Extra-virgin olive oil, for drizzling
Salt
2 slices homemade bread, cut into ¾-inch/2-cm cubes (optional)

Pour 68 fl oz/8 cups/2 liters cold water into a large saucepan, add the lentils, bring to a boil, then reduce the heat and simmer for 15 minutes. Drain and set aside.

Meanwhile, add the lardo, garlic, chopped parsley, and diced tomatoes to another pan and season with salt. Add 34 fl oz/4 cups/1 liter water and bring to a boil.

Add the drained lentils to the pan, stir, and cook over a low heat for 5–10 minutes, taking care not to overcook them. Remove the pan from the heat and drizzle two to three times with extra-virgin olive oil.

Meanwhile, if desired, heat a drizzle of oil in a skillet (frying pan), add the bread cubes, and fry for 3 minutes, or until toasted all over.

Serve the lentil soup piping hot, and topped with the croutons, if using.

Stringozzi with mushrooms and truffles

A similar shape to fettucine, stringozzi is an Umbrian specialty made from only flour and water. The simplicity of the pasta is enhanced by the accompanying mushrooms and black truffles.

PREPARATION TIME 45 minutes

COOKING TIME 20 minutes

SERVES 6

1¾ fl oz/scant ¼ cup/50 ml olive oil

2 cloves garlic, peeled and left whole

3½ ounces/100 g guanciale (cured pork cheek), cut into strips

7 ounces/200 g fresh mushrooms, sliced

Pinch of crumbled dried red chile

3½ ounces/100 g black truffles, grated

2–3 tomatoes, skinned and chopped

1 pound 5 ounces/5 cups/600 g all-purpose (plain) flour

Salt and black pepper

Grated pecorino cheese, to serve

Heat the oil in a large skillet (frying pan), add the garlic, and sauté until golden brown, then remove from the pan and discard. Add the guanciale to the pan and sauté for 1 minute, then add the sliced mushrooms and stir in the crumbled chile. Add the truffles and tomatoes and cook for about 10 minutes. Adjust the seasoning with salt and pepper, then remove the pan from the heat and leave to rest.

To make the pasta dough, gather the flour into a mound on a clean work surface and make a well in the center. Add lukewarm water, a little at a time, to the well and mix until a dough forms. Knead the dough until it is smooth and compact, then roll it out into a slightly thicker sheet. Roll it up into a log and cut out relatively wide tagliatelle-like strips, then cut into shorter lengths, about ¼ inch/5 mm wide and 12 inches/30 cm long, typical of stringozzi.

Cook the pasta in a large saucepan of boiling salted water for 2–3 minutes, or until al dente, then quickly drain. Add the pasta to the tomato sauce and sauté for 2 minutes. Serve with grated pecorino cheese.

Umbrian spring vegetable soup

Scafata

This springtime soup features seasonal garden vegetables such as scallions (spring onions), carrots, fava (broad) beans, and Swiss chard, and takes its name—*scafata*—from the local term for fava bean pods.

PREPARATION TIME 25 minutes

COOKING TIME 40–45 minutes

SERVES 4

2 tablespoons extra-virgin olive oil
1 ounce/30 g lardo battuto (lardo paste with garlic and herbs)
2 carrots, coarsely chopped
1 scallion (spring onion), coarsely chopped
10½ ounces/300 g fava (broad) beans, shelled and peeled
2 tomatoes, diced
Vegetable stock, for cooking
5½ ounces/150 g Swiss chard leaves, torn
Salt and black pepper
Slices of bread, lightly toasted, to serve (optional)

Heat the oil in a large saucepan with a lid over a low heat, add the lardo battuto, carrots, and scallion (spring onion), and sauté until the lardo turns translucent and the vegetables lightly color. Add the fava (broad) beans and diced tomatoes. Season sparingly with salt and sauté for another 1–2 minutes. Add enough vegetable stock to cover the contents of the pan and bring to a boil. Cover with a lid and cook over a medium heat for 10–15 minutes.

Add the chard and continue to cook for 20–25 minutes until the fava beans are tender. Turn off the heat and leave to rest for a few minutes before serving with the toasted bread, if desired.

Stuffed pheasant

Umbria produces more black truffles than anywhere else in Italy, and here—along with mushrooms, prosciutto, and cheese—they are used to stuff a pheasant, another common ingredient of the region.

PREPARATION TIME 30 minutes
COOKING TIME 1 hour 40 minutes
SOAKING TIME 1 hour
SERVES 4

½ ounce/scant ⅔ cup/15 g dried porcini mushrooms
1 × 2 pound 4 ounce/1 kg pheasant or guinea fowl
1 egg
3½ ounces/100 g prosciutto, cut into strips
1 medium black truffle, grated, or 1 tube black truffle paste
3½ ounces/generous ¾ cup/100 g grated Grana Padano cheese
¾ ounce/1½ tablespoons/20 g unsalted butter
Vegetable oil, for cooking
1 sprig rosemary
A few fresh sage leaves
5 fl oz/⅔ cup/150 ml good-quality dry white wine
Hot meat broth (stock), for cooking (optional)
Salt and black pepper

Soak the dried mushrooms in a bowl of hot water for 1 hour.

Preheat the oven to 400 °F/200 °C/180 °C Fan/Gas 6.

Bone the pheasant, then cut up the carcass and set aside. Lay the bird on a work surface and, using a meat mallet, beat the flesh until thin, then season with salt on both sides.

Drain and squeeze out the mushrooms to remove the excess liquid, then coarsely chop. Add them to a bowl with the egg, prosciutto, truffle, and cheese. Season with a little salt and plenty of pepper and mix everything well to combine.

Stuff the pheasant with the mixture, sew up the opening, and tie up the bird with kitchen twine (string).

Heat the butter with a few tablespoons of oil and the rosemary and sage in a large ovenproof pan. Add the pheasant and brown evenly. Pour in the wine and stir to scrape up all the crispy bits off the bottom of the pan. Add the carcass pieces to the pan, cover with aluminum foil, and cook in the preheated oven for 1 hour 15 minutes, or until the internal temperature of the pheasant reaches 160°F/71°C on a meat thermometer. Remove the foil and cook for another 15 minutes, adding a little hot broth (stock) if necessary while cooking, to keep things moist.

Remove the pan from the oven and leave the pheasant to cool. Strain the sauce and reduce it over the heat until thick, if necessary. Carve the pheasant into slices, arrange them in a serving dish, and serve with the piping-hot sauce separately.

Pork loin with juniper

A perfect Sunday lunch dish, the pork loin is wrapped in pancetta slices, giving it a wonderful texture and flavor, while the marinade of white wine, onion, and juniper berries gives the dish its characteristic aroma.

PREPARATION TIME 25 minutes
COOKING TIME 1 hour
MARINATING TIME 2 hours
RESTING TIME 5 minutes
SERVES 4

1 onion, chopped
10 juniper berries, lightly crushed
1 dried bay leaf
4–6 tablespoons extra-virgin olive oil
1¾ fl oz/scant ¼ cup/50 ml dry white wine
1 pound 12 ounces/800 g pork loin, silver skin trimmed off
3½ ounces/100 g pancetta, sliced
Salt and black pepper

Combine the onion, juniper berries, and bay leaf in a large bowl with 2–3 tablespoons of the oil and the wine. Season with salt and pepper and mix well. Place the pork loin in an ovenproof dish and pour over two-thirds of the marinade, setting the remainder aside. Cover with plastic wrap (cling film) and leave to marinate in the refrigerator for 2 hours, turning the meat over after the first hour.

Drain the meat and pat dry with paper towels, then wrap the loin in the pancetta, partly overlapping the slices so that the whole piece of meat is well covered. Tie the loin with kitchen string to compact.

Preheat the oven to 350 °F/180 °C/160 °C Fan/Gas 4. Line the ovenproof dish with parchment paper.

Add the remaining 2–3 tablespoons of oil to the prepared dish and add the loin. Roast in the preheated oven for 1 hour, or until its internal temperature reaches 158 °F/70 °C on a meat thermometer. While roasting, baste the meat with a few tablespoons of the leftover marinade from time to time. Once the meat is cooked, remove it from the oven and leave it to rest for 5 minutes to settle and cool before serving.

Festive meringue cake

Ciaramicola

Typical of Perugia, the capital of the region, this festive cake is traditionally made on Good Friday and eaten on Easter Sunday. The red batter and white meringue represent the colors of the city's coat of arms.

PREPARATION TIME 45 minutes

COOKING TIME 1 hour 20 minutes

SERVES 10–12

4 ounces/1 stick/120 g butter, melted and cooled, plus extra
    for greasing
1 pound 2 ounces/generous 4 cups/500 g Italian "00" flour,
    plus extra for dusting
½ ounce/16 g baking powder
4 eggs, at room temperature
10½ ounces/1⅓ cups/300 g superfine (caster) sugar
5½ fl oz/⅔ cup/160 ml Alchermes liqueur
1 tablespoon grated orange zest
Colored sprinkles, to decorate

FOR THE MERINGUE
3½ ounces/100 g (about 3) egg whites, at room temperature
3½ ounces/scant ½ cup/100 g superfine (caster) sugar
3½ ounces/generous ¾ cup/100 g confectioners' (icing) sugar

Preheat the oven to 350 °F/180 °C/160 °C Fan/Gas 4. Grease a 10½-inch/26-cm ring cake pan (tin) with butter and add a dusting of flour.

Sift the flour and baking powder into a large bowl. Place the eggs and sugar in a large bowl and beat with an electric whisk until pale and fluffy. Add the melted butter and liqueur and stir in.

Add the sifted flour mixture and the grated orange zest and mix well to combine, then transfer the batter to the prepared cake pan and level the surface. Bake in the preheated oven for 45 minutes. Check that the cake is cooked by inserting a toothpick (cocktail stick) into the center and if it comes out clean, the cake is done. Remove it from the oven and leave to cool completely.

Reduce the oven temperature to 195 °F/90 °C/70 °C Fan/ Gas ¼.

Meanwhile, for the meringue, add the egg whites to a large bowl and whisk with an electric whisk until they start to turn white. Sprinkle in the superfine (caster) sugar and beat for 2 minutes, then sprinkle in the confectioners' (icing) sugar and continue whisking until it forms a glossy and thick meringue with stiff peaks.

Using a spoon, spread the meringue over the top of the cake, still in the cake pan, and decorate with colored sprinkles. Bake in the preheated oven for 35–40 minutes until the meringue hardens. Remove from the oven and leave to cool before very carefully removing it from the cake pan onto a cooling rack, then set aside to cool completely before serving.

Sweet walnut tagliatelle

Tagliatelle dolci alle noci

This sweet pasta dish with walnuts and chocolate is a recipe that has passed down the generations. It is served as a dessert on holiday occasions—on the eve of All Saints' Day and at Christmas time.

PREPARATION TIME 20 minutes

COOKING TIME 10 minutes

SERVES 4

1 ounce/scant ¼ cup/30 shelled walnuts
2½ ounces/scant ⅓ cup/70 g superfine (caster) sugar
¾ ounce/scant ¼ cup/25 g unsweetened cocoa powder
1 ounce/⅔ cup/30 g bread crumbs
Grated zest of 1 lemon
Pinch of ground cinnamon (optional)
10½ ounces/300 g tagliatelle
Salt

Preheat the oven to 325 °F/160 °C/140 °C Fan/Gas 3.

Briefly cook the walnuts in a saucepan of water for a few minutes, then drain, peel, and dry them on a baking sheet in the preheated oven. Transfer the walnuts to a chopping board and coarsely chop them together with the sugar, cocoa, bread crumbs, grated lemon zest, and the cinnamon, if using.

Meanwhile, cook the pasta in a large saucepan of boiling salted water for 10 minutes, or until al dente. Drain, transfer to a serving dish, and add the walnut mixture. Mix well, then set the pasta aside to cool to room temperature before serving.

Lazio

Carciofi alla giudia and Castelli wines

Lazio, Latium, is home to Rome. And just a stone's throw away you will find the castle towns, known as the castelli. Both are deeply connected culinary realities with strong flavors, and the more precise these flavors are, the more delectable they become. There is the Rome of shepherds, which clings to its ancestral lamb and kid goat roasts; the Rome of vignarola, spring vegetables, with its stewed peas and fava (broad) beans, and fragrant salads of mixed greens and curly puntarelle with anchovies (page 199); and gluttonous Rome, where every part of the city is filled with rigatoni and bucatini. In the old neighborhoods you will find carciofi alla giudia (page 190), and the famous saltimbocca (page 200). On the way to the castelli, mushrooms add an earthy fragrance to the fettuccine, just as real milk gives its aroma to the ricotta and ricottina cheeses still sold in baskets. And above all else is porchetta, a specialty of Ariccia. Lazio still has the smell of woods, countryside, and vineyards, of pecorino cheese with fava beans, of lettuces, chicory, and endives, and of the strawberries grown in Nemi. The white wines of Frascati, Orvieto, and Montefiascone are sipped outdoors under a pergola, or indoors in one of the many trattoria, and in small city restaurants overlooking squares, almost always facing a church or fountain.

Jewish-style fried artichokes

Carciofi alla giudia

These twice-fried artichokes, known for their flower-like appearance, have their roots in Roman-Jewish cuisine, and are served in every restaurant in Rome's historical Ghetto neighborhood.

PREPARATION TIME 40 minutes

COOKING TIME 25 minutes

SERVES 4

4 tender globe artichokes
Juice of 2 lemons
50 fl oz/6¼ cups/1.5 liters peanut (groundnut) oil, for deep-frying
Salt and black pepper

First trim the artichokes by removing all the outer, darker and harder leaves, leaving only the lighter ones. Peel and trim the stalk and the base of the artichoke where the leaves were initially attached. Cut off the tips of the remaining leaves. As they are trimmed, place the artichokes in a large bowl of water with the lemon juice. When ready, drain the artichokes and wipe them dry with paper towels.

Heat the oil for deep-frying in a large, deep saucepan to 350 °F/180 °C, or until a cube of bread browns in 30 seconds. Carefully add the artichokes to the hot oil and deep-fry for about 10 minutes. Prick the artichokes with a fork to check that they are cooked: it should pierce the heart easily. Remove the artichokes from the oil and set aside to cool and drain upside down on a plate. Once cool, open the leaves as to give them a flower-like appearance.

Return the artichokes, leaf side down, to the oil for 2 minutes, lightly pressing them against the bottom of the pan. Remove them from the oil and leave them upside down on a plate lined with paper towels. Season the artichokes with salt and pepper and serve while still hot.

Spaghetti carbonara

Spaghetti alla carbonara

One of the great classics of Italian cuisine—yet everyone has their own beloved recipe. The traditional Roman version is given below, and should be made with the best quality artisanal pasta you can find.

PREPARATION TIME 20 minutes

COOKING TIME 20 minutes

SERVES 4

10½ ounces/300 g aged guanciale (cured pork cheek), cut into cubes

5 egg yolks

2 ounces/scant ⅔ cup/50 g grated Pecorino Romano (PDO) cheese with black rind, grated, plus extra to serve

11 ounces/320 g spaghetti

Salt and black pepper

Sauté the guanciale (cured pork cheek) in a large skillet (frying pan) until colored. No oil is needed, as the guanciale will release its own fat as it cooks. Turn off the heat and drain the excess fat into a bowl. Strain the fat through a fine-mesh strainer (sieve) into another bowl.

Add the egg yolks to a metal bowl with the guanciale fat and beat together with a whisk. Bring a large saucepan of water to a boil. Set the bowl of egg yolks over the pan, making sure the bottom of the bowl doesn't touch the water, and beat. Add the cheese and stir until it is incorporated, then remove the bowl from the heat. If you find the sauce is too thick, stir in a few tablespoons of hot water until the mixture is glossy and creamy.

Cook the spaghetti in a large saucepan of boiling lightly salted water for 10 minutes, or until al dente, then add it to the guanciale. Turn on the heat and mix the pasta with the guanciale for a few minutes. Transfer the contents of the pan to a heated soup tureen. Add the sauce, season with pepper, and mix well.

Divide the spaghetti between serving plates and top with grated cheese and a sprinkling of pepper. It is now ready to be served.

Mozzarella sandwich

A tasty finger-food dish of deep-fried stringy mozzarella encased in sandwich bread—literally *in carozza*, meaning "in a carriage"—the dish started out as a means of using up leftover bread and cheese.

PREPARATION TIME 10 minutes

COOKING TIME 15 minutes

RESTING TIME 1 hour

SERVES 4–6

12 slices white sandwich bread, crusts trimmed off
1 (9-ounce/250-g) ball mozzarella di bufala cheese, sliced
All-purpose (plain) flour, for coating
5 eggs
Bread crumbs, for coating
Peanut (groundnut) oil, for deep-frying
Pinch of salt

Cover half of the bread slices with the cheese, leaving a little margin around the edges unfilled. Season them lightly with salt. Close each sandwich with its corresponding bread slice and press on them with the palm of your hand to compact. Cut them into triangles.

Sift some flour onto a plate, beat the eggs in a shallow dish, and spread some bread crumbs out on another plate. Toss the sandwiches in the sifted flour, making sure that the edges are also well coated, then dip them into the eggs, and finally, toss them in the bread crumbs. Leave the sandwiches to firm up in the refrigerator for 30 minutes.

Repeat the coating process a second time, without dredging the sandwiches in flour, only dipping them into the egg and then into the bread crumbs. Refrigerate them for another 30 minutes.

Heat enough oil for deep-frying in a large, deep saucepan to 344 °F/170 °C on a thermometer, or until a bread cube browns in 30 seconds. Add the sandwiches and deep-fry until they turn golden brown. Using a slotted spoon, remove the sandwiches from the oil and drain on paper towels. Serve immediately.

Spaghetti with cheese and pepper

To make this dish truly authentic, the pepper must be freshly ground and plentiful, and the cheese must be Pecorino Romano (PDO), which has the unique ability to melt in hot water to form the creamy sauce.

PREPARATION TIME 5 minutes

COOKING TIME 8–10 minutes

SERVES 4

2 tablespoons black peppercorns
7 ounces/1⅔ cups/200 g grated Pecorino Romano (PDO) cheese
11½ ounces/320 g spaghetti or tonnarelli
Salt and black pepper

Grind the peppercorns to a fine powder in a mortar and pestle. Add the grated cheese to a large bowl with the pepper.

Cook the pasta in a large saucepan of boiling salted water for 8–10 minutes While the pasta is cooking, gradually add some of the pasta cooking water to the bowl with the cheese and stir vigorously with a whisk to a creamy sauce. When the pasta is al dente, drain, and add it to the bowl with the sauce and mix until well coated.

Divide the pasta between serving plates, add a sprinkling of freshly ground pepper, and serve.

Bucatini all'Amatriciana

There are many interpretations of this iconic Italian starter dish, but the traditional version features bucatini, tomatoes, guanciale, and pecorino, and is named for the hill town of Amatrice.

PREPARATION TIME 15 minutes

COOKING TIME 25 minutes

SERVES 4

10½ ounces/300 g tomatoes (4–5 very ripe tomatoes when in season)
1 tablespoon extra-virgin olive oil
4 ounces/120 g thickly sliced guanciale (cured pork cheek), cut into strips
1 fresh red chile
1¾ fl oz/scant ¼ cup/50 ml dry and tart white wine
11 ounces/320 g bucatini (or spaghetti or spaghettoni)
About 2 ounces/scant ⅔ cup/50 g grated pecorino cheese (mild and not too salty)
Salt and black pepper

Add the tomatoes to a large saucepan of boiling salted water and blanch for 90 seconds, then drain and refresh them under cold running water. Once they are cool enough to handle, remove the skins, cut the tomatoes in half, remove the seeds, and cut the tomato flesh into strips.

Heat the oil in a large cast-iron skillet (frying pan), add the guanciale (cured pork cheek), and sauté until the fat starts to melt.

Add the chile and sauté until it colors, then pour in the wine and stir, scraping up all the crispy bits from the bottom of the pan. Allow the wine to evaporate, then drain the guanciale, set aside, and keep warm.

Cook the pasta in a large saucepan of boiling salted water for 10 minutes, or until al dente.

Meanwhile, put the tomatoes into the same skillet where the guanciale was cooked, adjust the seasoning with salt, and cook for as long as it takes the pasta to cook.

When the sauce is almost cooked, add the guanciale, and remove and discard the chile. Drain the pasta and add it to the pan with the sauce. Remove from the heat, add the grated cheese, and adjust the seasoning with pepper. Serve immediately.

Puntarelle salad

This traditional Roman dish features puntarelle, the sprouts of the Catalogna chicory, cut into strips and soaked in iced water to remove some of their bitterness, topped with an anchovy dressing.

PREPARATION TIME 30 minutes
SOAKING TIME 1 hour
SERVES 4

1 pound 5 ounces/600 g puntarelle, well cleaned
4 salt-packed anchovy fillets, boned
1 clove garlic, crushed
Extra-virgin olive oil
White wine vinegar, for the dressing
Salt and black pepper

Separate the large inner shoots from the outer leaves of the puntarelle, then separate the individual shoots, trim off the bases, and cut them in half lengthwise. Cut each shoot into strips.

Soak the strips for about 1 hour in a bowl of ice water, then drain thoroughly while you make the anchovy dressing.

Soak the anchovies in a bowl of water for 5–20 minutes, then drain and cut them into small pieces. Place them in a bowl with the crushed garlic and oil and, using a fork, mix together while pouring enough vinegar in a thin, steady stream to form an emulsion. Adjust the seasoning with a pinch of salt, if necessary.

Transfer the puntarelle strips to a serving dish and toss them with the anchovy dressing. Season with a sprinkling of pepper and serve.

Roman-style saltimbocca

One of Lazio's best-known dishes, saltimbocca consists of slices of veal topped with prosciutto and a sage leaf, lightly dredged in flour before cooking in butter to create a light crust.

PREPARATION TIME 20 minutes

COOKING TIME 15 minutes

SERVES 4

14 ounces/400 g slices lean veal, cut into even-size pieces
  (not too small)
3½ ounces/100 g prosciutto
Fresh sage leaves (1 leaf for each piece of veal)
Italian "00" flour, for coating
2 ounces/3½ tablespoons/50 g unsalted butter
Dry white wine, for deglazing
Salt and black pepper

Cover each piece of meat with half a slice of prosciutto, then top each one with a sage leaf and secure with a toothpick (cocktail stick).

Spread some flour out on a large plate and toss each piece of veal until lightly coated, shaking off the excess. Heat the butter in a large skillet (frying pan), add the meat, and fry for a few minutes on both sides. Adjust the seasoning with salt, pour in a generous splash of wine and stir, scraping up all the crispy bits on the bottom of the pan, then allow it to evaporate.

Finish with a sprinkling of pepper, then remove from the heat and immediately serve the saltimbocca piping hot with the sauce from the pan.

Maritozzi

The maritozzo is a traditional pastry typical of the Lazio region, particularly Rome. The classic recipe calls for the addition of orange zest, and these soft, sweet rolls are served filled with whipped cream.

PREPARATION TIME 20 minutes
COOKING TIME 15–20 minutes
RISING TIME 6 hours
MAKES 6

FOR THE STARTER DOUGH
¼ ounce/5 g fresh yeast
1 teaspoon superfine (caster) sugar
2 ounces/scant ½ cup/50 g Italian "00" flour

FOR THE DOUGH
1 egg yolk
2 ounces/scant ¼ cup/50 g superfine (caster) sugar
¾ fl oz/4 teaspoons/20 ml milk
1½ fl oz/3 tablespoons/40 ml seed oil

7 ounces/1⅔ cups/200 g Manitoba flour (strong white bread flour)
Grated zest of 1 orange

FOR THE EGG WASH
1 egg yolk
1 tablespoon milk

FOR THE FILLING
7 fl oz/scant 1 cup/200 ml whipping cream

For the starter dough, add the yeast, sugar, and Italian "00" flour to a large bowl, then pour in 1¾ fl oz/scant ¼ cup/50 ml water and stir until the yeast and sugar have dissolved. Cover with plastic wrap (cling film) and leave to rise for about 1 hour.

In another bowl, for the dough, combine the egg yolk, sugar, milk, oil, and Manitoba flour. Add the starter, followed by the orange zest, and mix, then knead until the dough is a soft and elastic consistency. Cover and leave the dough to rise in a warm place for at least 4 hours.

Once the dough has risen, line a large baking sheet with parchment paper. Shape the dough into slightly elongated buns, place them on the prepared baking sheet, and leave them to proof for at least 40–50 minutes.

Preheat the oven to 350 °F/180 °C/160 °C Fan/Gas 4.

For the egg wash, add the egg yolk and milk to a bowl and stir to combine, then use to brush the buns all over. Bake in the preheated oven for 15–20 minutes. Transfer the buns to a cooling rack and leave them to cool completely.

Meanwhile, for the filling, whip the cream in a bowl with an electric whisk or in a stand mixer fitted with a whisk attachment until stiff peaks form. Using a serrated knife, cut the buns in half lengthwise down the center without going through them completely. Open them slightly, spoon in some whipped cream, and serve.

South

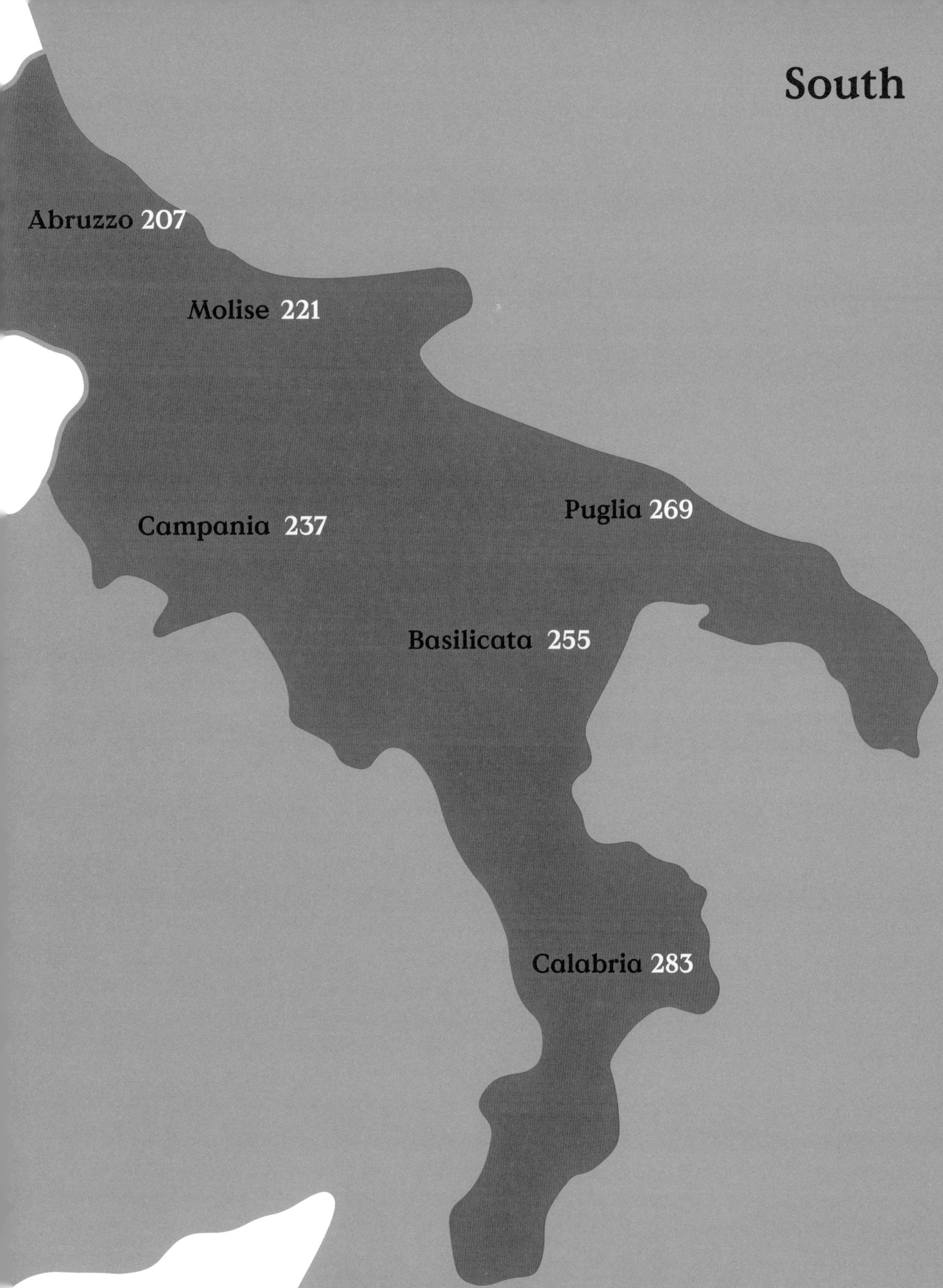

Abruzzo **207**

Molise **221**

Campania **237**

Puglia **269**

Basilicata **255**

Calabria **283**

Abruzzo

Where cooking is still what it used to be

We keenly sample the flavors of Abruzzo, a region that for decades remained remote and secret, before opening up to a healthy and lively tourism which discovered the wonders of its isolated mountains and long, sandy coastlines. This task was completed by the appeal of its food. Following the aromas hovering in the air, holidaymakers came across unimagined assortments of produce of astonishing quality, and food products made in the old-fashioned way. Abruzzo is a region where sheep farming is still a tradition and, consequently, where you will find lamb, mutton, and kid goat meat cooked with olives, seasoned with lemon juice or vinegar, or stewed, as well as artfully made cheeses such as Pecorino di Farindola. The same expertise goes into the rearing of pigs, resulting in such rarities as the tasty Campotosto mortadella and Ventricina di Vasto to delight the palate. On the Navelli Plateau, nature works its wonders through saffron, whose threads are as precious as gold—or maybe even more so. And in the Fara San Martino district, the waters of the River Verde are ideal for making durum wheat pasta that is delicious even unflavored. From Martinsicuro to Vasto, the sea is filled with fish, all of which goes into the stew known as brodetto. Finally, it is a surprise to find that so many homes still have a larder where the flavors of tradition are preserved, while bottles of red Montepulciano and white Trebbiano rest in cellars.

Chitarra with meatballs

Chitarra is a square-section spaghetti-style pasta named for the traditional rectangular wooden frame with parallel wires used to make it, which resembles a guitar (*chitarra*).

PREPARATION TIME 1 hour
COOKING TIME 1 hour 40 minutes
RESTING TIME 30 minutes
SERVES 4

7 ounces/1⅔ cups/200 g Italian "00" flour
7 ounces/generous 1 cup/200 g fine semolina
4 large eggs
Salt and black pepper

FOR THE SAUCE
5 tablespoons olive oil
1 onion, chopped
1 pound 5 ounces/600 g ripe tomatoes, skinned, seeded, and chopped
1 sprig parsley, finely chopped

FOR THE MEATBALLS
7 ounces/200 g ground (minced) veal
7 ounces/200 g ground (minced) chicken breast
1 egg yolk
2 ounces/½ cup/50 g grated Grana Padano cheese
Pinch of grated nutmeg
Olive oil, for cooking

To make the pasta, gather both flours in a mound on a clean work surface and make a well in the center. Add the eggs to the well, followed by a little salt, and knead to a smooth and compact dough. Gather the dough into a ball, then wrap in plastic wrap (cling film) and leave to rest at room temperature for 30 minutes.

Using a rolling pin, roll the dough out on a clean work surface to a relatively thin sheet, then cut it into 6×12-inch/15×30-cm sheets. One at a time, lay the sheets on a *chitarra* ("guitar") pasta cutter and press with the rolling pin so that the strings cut the sheet into spaghetti strands.

To make the sauce, heat the oil in a large saucepan, add the onion, and sauté until it turns translucent. Add the chopped tomatoes and parsley, season with salt and pepper, and cook for about 1 hour, or until the sauce thickens.

Meanwhile, make the meatballs. In a large bowl, mix the ground (minced) meats with the egg yolk and cheese, and season with a pinch each of nutmeg, salt, and pepper. Take a small amount of the mixture at a time and shape it into small balls, about ½–¾ inch/1–2 cm in diameter.

Line a plate with paper towels. Heat a little oil in a large skillet (frying pan) and fry the meatballs for a few minutes. Remove with a slotted spoon and leave to drain on the paper towels. You may need to cook them in batches. Add the meatballs to the sauce and cook for 5 minutes.

Meanwhile, cook the pasta in a large saucepan of water for 10 minutes, or until al dente. Drain, add to the sauce, and mix well. Serve.

"The seven virtues" minestrone

A hearty dish from Teramo, traditionally served on May Day using the leftover vegetables and legumes (pulses) discovered when spring cleaning the pantry— ideally seven of each to represent the seven virtues.

PREPARATION TIME 1 hour
COOKING TIME 3 hours
SOAKING TIME 12 hours
SERVES 6

1 pound 2 ounces/2¾ cups/500 g mixture of dried chickpeas, lentils, fava (broad) beans, peas
10½ ounces/300 g mixture of spinach, carrots, zucchini (courgettes), Swiss chard, endive, lettuce
5½ ounces/150 g prosciutto bone
5½ ounces/150 g pork rind
3-ounce/80-g slice lardo (cured pork back fat), chopped
1 clove garlic, peeled and left whole
1 onion, chopped
1 sprig parsley
2 fresh ripe tomatoes, skinned, seeded, and chopped
1 celery stalk
9 ounces/250 g mixture of dried pasta and homemade egg pasta
Grated pecorino or Parmesan cheese, to serve

Soak the dried beans in separate bowls of water overnight.

The next day, drain, place them in separate saucepans, cover with water, and bring to a boil. Boil until they are half-cooked, then drain and set aside.

Place all the leaf vegetables together in a large saucepan. Cover with water and bring to a boil. Boil for a few minutes, then drain, squeeze out any excess liquid, and set aside.

Place the prosciutto bone and pork rind in another pan, cover with water, and bring to a boil. Simmer for 90 minutes, then take out the bone and scrape off and collect any remaining meat. Drain the pork rind and cut it into squares. Strain the resulting stock through a fine-mesh strainer (sieve) lined with cheesecloth (muslin) into a large pan.

To make the soffritto, add the lardo to another pan over low heat. Add the garlic and sauté until colored, then remove and discard it. Add the onion, parsley, and tomatoes, and cook for 15 minutes, then remove the pan from the heat.

Add the meat and pork rind, the soffritto, and boiled leaf vegetables to the pan with the stock. Cook for 10 minutes, then add the pasta, chickpeas, fava (broad) beans, lentils, and peas and cook through. Remove from the heat, transfer the minestrone to a soup tureen, and serve with grated cheese.

Turnips and beans

When the cold winter months arrive in Abruzzo, this traditional peasant-style dish combines turnips and dried beans in a tasty, nutritious, and warming meal.

PREPARATION TIME 30 minutes
COOKING TIME 1 hour 20 minutes
SOAKING TIME 12 hours
SERVES 6

14 ounces/scant 2¼ cups/400 g dried borlotti beans
4 pounds 8 ounces/2 kg turnips, peeled and cut into thirds
2 cloves garlic, peeled and left whole
1 small piece of chile
2 fl oz/¼ cup/60 ml olive oil, plus extra for drizzling
Salt

Soak the dried beans in a large bowl of water overnight.

The next day, drain the beans, transfer to a large saucepan, cover with water, and bring to a boil. Boil the beans for 1 hour. Season with salt only at the end.

Cook the turnips in another large saucepan of boiling salted water for 10 minutes, then drain well.

Heat the oil in a pan (preferably a terracotta cooking pot), add the garlic and chile, and sauté until the garlic turns golden. Remove and discard the garlic and chile. Add the well-drained turnips and beans and cook for about 10 minutes. Remove the pan from the heat, transfer the turnips and beans to a serving dish, and drizzle with oil.

Lamb skewers

Arrosticini

A well-known Abruzzo dish, these simple skewers
feature the subtle, sweet-tasting lamb and mutton
so prevalent in the region's cuisine, from the sheep
that graze wild across the hills and mountains.

PREPARATION TIME 30 minutes

COOKING TIME 10 minutes

SERVES 6

6 tablespoons olive oil
4 tablespoons white wine vinegar
2 pounds/1 kg boned leg of mutton or lamb,
   cut into 48 small cubes
Salt

Preheat the oven to its highest temperature setting.

If using wooden skewers, soak 12 in a bowl of water for at
least 5 minutes to prevent them burning while cooking.

Place the oil and vinegar in a bowl and whisk to an
emulsion. Season with salt.

Thread 4 mutton cubes onto each skewer, then place
them on a rack and cook in the preheated oven for
about 3 minutes. Baste the skewers with the emulsion
and cook for another 3–4 minutes.

Serve immediately.

Pork "cif e ciaf"

The expression "*cif e ciaf*" comes from the sound made by meat cooking as it is quickly turned in a frying pan. This dish is said to have originated in Chieti, where today there is still a museum dedicated to the pig.

PREPARATION TIME 15 minutes
COOKING TIME 30 minutes
SERVES 6

3½ fl oz/scant ½ cup/100 ml olive oil
3 cloves garlic, peeled and left whole
1 onion, thinly sliced
1 pound 12 ounces/800 g pork (traditionally, ribs are preferred), cut into medium-sized pieces
2 tablespoons chopped parsley
2 tablespoons chopped marjoram
Salt and black pepper
Slices of toasted bread, to serve

Heat a large skillet (frying pan), preferably cast iron, and add the oil. Add the garlic and thinly sliced onion and sauté until the onion is lightly colored. Add the meat, stir, and cook until the meat is well browned on all sides. Add the chopped parsley and marjoram, season with salt and pepper, and cook for about 10 minutes, or until the meat is well cooked, tasty, and tender (the time varies depending on the size of the pieces of meat). Remove from the heat, transfer to a serving dish, and serve with toasted bread drizzled with the pan juices.

Chocolate and almond tart

An iconic Abruzzo sweet treat, these delicious crispy tartlets have a soft filling of chocolate, almonds, and—traditionally—a jam made with the local Montepulciano grapes.

PREPARATION TIME 50 minutes

COOKING TIME 30 minutes

RESTING TIME 2 hours

SERVES 6–8

10½ ounces/2½ cups/300 g all-purpose (plain) flour, plus extra for dusting
1 teaspoon baking powder
3 egg yolks
4 ounces/½ cup/120 g superfine (caster) sugar
5 ounces/generous ¾ cup/150 g lard, softened
Grated zest of 1 lemon

FOR THE FILLING
7 ounces/200 g dark chocolate, grated
5 ounces/generous 1 cup/150 g almonds, toasted and finely chopped
5 tablespoons grape jam
Grated zest of 1 lemon
1 teaspoon ground cinnamon
¾ fl oz/4 teaspoons/20 ml mosto cotto (grape juice syrup)
Confectioners' (icing) sugar, for dusting

Sift the flour and baking powder together in a bowl. Place the egg yolks and superfine (caster) sugar in another large bowl and beat together. Add the lard, the sifted flour and baking powder, and the grated lemon zest and knead briefly to form a soft dough. Wrap the dough in plastic wrap (cling film) and leave to rest for 2 hours in the refrigerator.

Meanwhile, make the filling. Mix the chocolate, finely chopped almonds, jam, lemon zest, cinnamon, and the mosto cotto (grape juice) together in a large bowl until combined.

Preheat the oven to 350 °F/180 °C/160 °C Fan/Gas 4. Dust 6–8 tartlet pans (tins), about 4 inches/10 cm, with flour.

Roll out the dough on a floured work surface. Using a cookie cutter, cut out small disks and use to line the prepared tartlet pans. Spread 1 tablespoon of the filling onto the base of the pastry and top with another pastry disk. Press well around the edges to seal. Repeat until all the ingredients are used up.

Bake the tartlets in the preheated oven for 30 minutes. Remove from the oven and leave to cool still in the pans, then turn them out and dust with plenty of confectioners' (icing) sugar.

Pescaran-style Christmas cake

A dome-shaped, chocolate-covered Christmas cake invented in 1920 by baker Luigi d'Amico of Pescara, who was inspired to make a confectionery version of the yellow, wood-fired bread called pane rozzo.

PREPARATION TIME 30 minutes
COOKING TIME 45 minutes
SERVES 6

6 eggs
7 ounces/generous ¾ cup/200 g superfine (caster) sugar
7 ounces/1⅔ cups/200 g ground almonds
5 ounces/scant 1 cup/150 g semolina
Grated zest of 1 lemon
2 tablespoons almond-flavored liqueur (e.g. Amaretto di Saronno)
2 fl oz/¼ cup/60 ml olive oil
Unsalted butter, for greasing
All-purpose (plain) flour, for dusting

FOR THE FROSTING (ICING)
¾ ounce/1½ tablespoons/20 g unsalted butter
7 ounces/200 g dark chocolate, broken into pieces

Preheat the oven to 325 °F/160 °C/140 °C Fan/Gas 3.

Separate the eggs into two bowls. Add the sugar to the egg yolks and beat until pale and fluffy, then add the almonds, semolina, grated lemon zest, and liqueur. Beat the egg whites until stiff peaks form, then gently fold them into the batter.

Grease a hemisphere/dome-shaped cake pan (tin), about 8½ inches/22 cm (for the typical shape of this cake) with butter and dust with flour.

Add the batter to the prepared pan and bake in the preheated oven for 40–45 minutes. Check that the cake is cooked by inserting a toothpick (cocktail stick) into the center and if it comes out clean and dry, the cake is done. Leave the cake to cool in the pan for 10 minutes, then gently turn it out onto a cooling rack and leave it to cool completely.

To make the frosting (icing), melt the butter and chocolate in a heatproof bowl set over a small pan of simmering water. Don't let the bottom of the bowl touch the water. Spread the frosting over the top of the cake and set aside to cool before serving.

Molise

Tantalizing flavors of cheese and bruschetta

Molise, once a part of neighboring Abruzzo, is now definitively independent, though without having renounced its culinary kinship derived from long years of cohabitation. Examples of this include the skills for processing pork, which is made into charcuterie with the flavors of home—often chile or fennel—such as capocolli, ventricine, and soppressate, as well as sausages in oil or lard, an absolute marvel. It is also seen in how the sheep farming has been preserved through the use of modern methods. The result is superb ewe's milk cheeses, such as Pecorino di Capracotta and dishes such as agnello cac'e'ova (lamb with cheese and egg) from the Matese mountains, pezzata, an age-old stew, and turcinelli, balls of offal wrapped in intestines and broiled (grilled) or barbecued. Worthy of note is caciocavallo di Agnone cheese, which is eaten between spring and summer when it is at the peak of its goodness. What is more, because of its largely untouched forests, Molise is now Italy's largest producer of white truffles, protected by a special consortium. Naturally, all along the low-lying, sandy Adriatic coastline, the cuisine features a great variety of fish and seafood in a multitude of tasty dishes, with great demand for brodetto of all kinds (page 230). Where wine is concerned, the most important in the region is undoubtedly Biferno, which is made in red, rosé, and white versions.

Molise-style bruschetta

The most famous Molise appetizer, a wonderfully colorful and flavorful dish similar in style to bruschetta. Eggs, tomatoes, cucumber, olives, bell peppers, and celery are piled on taralli-style crackers.

PREPARATION TIME 40 minutes
RESTING TIME 30 minutes
SERVES 4

2 fl oz/¼ cup/60 ml olive oil
4 oil-packed anchovy fillets, drained and finely chopped
1 tablespoon dried oregano
4 Molise-style taralli (ring-shaped crackers)
4 teaspoons white wine vinegar
14 ounces/400 g very ripe tomatoes, seeded and sliced or halved
1 cucumber, peeled and thinly sliced
1 bell pepper, cored and thinly sliced
1 celery stalk, thinly sliced
2 hard-boiled eggs, sliced
8 green olives
8 black olives
Salt

In a bowl, mix the oil with the finely chopped anchovies. Add the oregano and season with salt.

Lightly moisten the crackers with a little cold water, sprinkle them with the vinegar, and leave them to dry on paper towels.

Arrange the crackers on the bottom of a serving dish and start to form layers on the top of them, starting with the tomatoes, then the cucumber, bell pepper, followed by the celery and finishing with the sliced eggs. Drizzle with the anchovy dressing and garnish with the green and black olives. Cover the dish with plastic wrap (cling film) and leave to chill in the refrigerator for 30 minutes before serving.

Baked wild chicory timbale

A one-pot dish of baked chicory and cheese—perfect for cold winter days. Scamorza is a traditional stretched curd cheese of the regions of southern Italy, including Molise, formed into a pear shape.

PREPARATION TIME 30 minutes
COOKING TIME 40 minutes
SERVES 4

2 pounds 4 ounces/1 kg wild chicory
Extra-virgin olive oil, for brushing and drizzling
1 Scamorza cheese, sliced
3 slices prosciutto, cut into strips
3 peeled tomatoes, cut into small pieces
1½ ounces/½ cup/40 g grated pecorino cheese
3 eggs
Salt

Preheat the oven to 350 °F/180 °C/160 °C Fan/Gas 4.

Remove any tough leaves from the chicory and cook the remaining leaves in a large saucepan of salted water for 10 minutes. Drain and squeeze out as much liquid as possible.

Line an 8-inch/20-cm round baking pan (tin) with waxed (greaseproof) paper, then brush it with oil. Carefully spread an even layer of chicory over the bottom. Cover the chicory with slices of cheese, then add another layer of chicory, followed by a layer of prosciutto and tomatoes. Cover them with more chicory and, finally, the grated pecorino cheese.

Beat the eggs with a pinch of salt in a small bowl, pour them over the timbale, and drizzle with oil. Bake the timbale in the preheated oven for 30 minutes, or until a golden crust has formed on the top. Remove from the oven, leave the timbale to rest for 5 minutes, then turn it out into a serving dish. Serve.

Molise-style fusilli

While this recipe can be made using shop-bought fusilli, you can also try making it by hand Molise-style, wrapping the dough of durum wheat flour, water, and salt around skewers to create a hollow pasta shape.

PREPARATION TIME 20 minutes

COOKING TIME 2 hours 20 minutes

SERVES 6

2¾ fl oz/⅓ cup/80 ml olive oil

1 onion, finely chopped

1 carrot, finely chopped

1 celery stalk, finely chopped

5 ounces/150 g lamb breast, cut into small pieces

7 ounces/200 g lean veal, cut into small pieces

2 sausages, chopped

3½ fl oz/scant ½ cup/100 ml red wine

1 pound 9 ounces/700 g tomatoes, skinned and cut into small pieces

14 ounces/400 g fusilli

Grated pecorino cheese, for sprinkling

Finely chopped parsley, for sprinkling

Salt

1 hot dried chile, crumbled, or chili flakes, to serve

Heat the oil in a large saucepan over a medium heat, add the onion, carrot, and celery, and sauté for 10 minutes. Add the lamb, veal, and sausages and cook until browned. Pour in the wine and allow it to evaporate. Add the tomatoes and salt to taste, then reduce the heat and cook for about 2 hours, stirring occasionally.

Cook the fusilli in a large saucepan of boiling salted water according to the package directions, then drain, transfer to a large serving dish, pour over the sauce, and sprinkle with grated pecorino cheese and chopped parsley. Serve with the chile to one side.

Vegetable wheel

Ruota di verdure

The essential ingredient in this ratatouille-style dish
is tomato, which imparts its flavor to everything else.
Try using shallots, eggplants (aubergines), or zucchini
(courgettes) in place of the potatoes and onions.

PREPARATION TIME 30 minutes

COOKING TIME 30 minutes

SERVES 4

4 tablespoons torn pieces of stale bread
Olive oil, for brushing and drizzling
4 large potatoes, peeled and cut into slices ½-inch/1-cm thick
3 white onions, cut into slices ½-inch/1-cm thick
3 large and fleshy tomatoes, cut into slices ½-inch/1-cm thick
Pinch of dried oregano
Salt

Preheat the oven to 350 °F/180 °C/160 °C Fan/Gas 4.

Blitz the bread in a food processor into crumbs.

Brush a round ovenproof dish with oil and arrange the
vegetables in concentric circles, alternating the potato,
onion, and tomato slices. Sprinkle everything with bread
crumbs and oregano and season with a drizzle of oil and
salt. Bake in the preheated oven for 30 minutes, or until
a light crust forms on the top. Remove from the oven and
leave it to rest for 10 minutes before serving.

Variation: Brush a round container with oil and arrange
the vegetables in layers, starting with the potatoes, then
the onions, and finally the tomatoes. Season each layer
with salt and oregano and add a sprinkling of bread
crumbs and a drizzle of oil. Repeat the process until all
the ingredients are used up, finishing with the tomatoes
seasoned with salt and oregano, sprinkled with bread
crumbs and drizzled with oil. Bake in the preheated
oven as described.

→ MOLISE

228

Molise fish stew

Once all the fish and shellfish have been eaten, the local custom in Molise is to add a few tablespoons of boiled pasta, such as tubetti or orecchiette, to the stew to soak up the remaining sauce.

PREPARATION TIME 50 minutes

COOKING TIME 35 minutes

SERVES 8–10

10½ ounces/300 g mussels, cleaned (page 323)
10½ ounces/300 g clams, cleaned (page 323)
1 tablespoon tomato paste (purée)
6 tablespoons olive oil
1 clove garlic, peeled and left whole
½ green bell pepper, cored, seeded, and cut into strips
1 red chile
14 ounces/400 g very ripe tomatoes, skinned, seeded,
    and chopped
10½ ounces/300 g small cuttlefish, skinned
5 pounds 8 ounces/2.5 kg fish of the same type or mixed (skate,
    cod, mullet, mackerel), gutted
10½ ounces/300 g mantis shrimp
1 sprig parsley, chopped
Salt

Place the mussels and clams in a large skillet (frying pan) over a high heat without any seasoning and cook until they open. Remove from the heat and discard any that remain closed.

In a small bowl, dilute the tomato paste (purée) with 2 ladlefuls of lukewarm water. Set aside. Heat the oil in a large saucepan (preferably a terracotta cooking pot), add the garlic, bell pepper, and chile, and sauté for a few minutes. Add the tomatoes and diluted tomato paste. Season with salt and bring to a boil for a few minutes.

Remove and discard the garlic, then start arranging layers of fish in the pan, starting with the less delicate ones, and adding the mussels, clams, and mantis shrimp at the end. Cook over a low heat for about 15 minutes. Just before cooking is finished, sprinkle the stew with chopped parsley. Serve it in the cooking pot.

St. Joseph's salt cod

Baccalà di San Giuseppe

The Adriatic coastline of the region ensures seafood dishes feature heavily in the local cuisine. This ancient salt cod recipe was one of thirteen meat-free dishes prepared to celebrate the feast of Saint Joseph.

PREPARATION TIME 30 minutes
COOKING TIME 30 minutes
SOAKING TIME 24 hours
SERVES 4

2 pounds 4 ounces/1 kg salt cod
2 tablespoons raisins
3½ fl oz/scant ½ cup/100 ml olive oil
1¼ ounces/½ cup/35 g dried bread crumbs
3 tablespoons shelled walnuts, chopped
2 cloves garlic, finely chopped
3 tablespoons chopped parsley
4 oil-packed anchovy fillets, drained and chopped
Salt

Soak the salt cod in a large bowl of water in the refrigerator for at least 24 hours, changing the water several times. Drain.

Preheat the oven to 325 °F/160 °C/140 °C Fan/Gas 3.

Place the raisins in a small bowl, cover with water, and leave to soak for 5 minutes. Drain and squeeze out the excess water.

Meanwhile, grease an ovenproof pan with a little of the oil. Cut the cod into uniform pieces and arrange them in a single layer in the pan.

Spread the bread crumbs over a baking sheet and toast in the preheated oven for a few minutes. Transfer them to a large bowl, add the walnuts, garlic, parsley, and anchovies, and soaked raisins. Season sparingly with salt, drizzle with a little more of the oil, and mix everything together.

Increase the oven temperature to 350 °F/180 °C/160 °C Fan/Gas 4.

Cover the cod with the bread crumb mixture. Drizzle everything with a little more oil and bake in the preheated oven for 30 minutes, or until a golden crust has formed on top.

Lamb fricassée with artichokes

A traditional main course of Molise. When cooking a fricassée, the recipe is completed with the addition of beaten eggs with lemon juice, creating a rich and luxurious creamy sauce.

PREPARATION TIME 20 minutes
COOKING TIME 1 hour 15 minutes
SERVES 4

2 tablespoons olive oil
½ onion, finely chopped
½ carrot, finely chopped
½ celery stalk, finely chopped
1 clove garlic, finely chopped
1 pound 14 ounces/800 g lamb shoulder, cut into pieces
1 tablespoon all-purpose (plain) flour
1¾ fl oz/scant ¼ cup/50 ml dry white wine
4 artichokes, trimmed and cut into wedges
2 eggs
Juice of 1 lemon
2 tablespoons chopped parsley
Salt and black pepper

Heat the oil in a large saucepan, add the chopped onion, carrot, celery, and garlic, and sauté for 5 minutes. Add the lamb pieces, sprinkle them with the flour, and cook until browned.

Pour the wine into the pan, stir to scrape up all the crispy bits off the bottom of the pan, and allow the wine to evaporate, then cook for 40 minutes. Remove from the heat, season with salt and pepper, and stir. Remove the meat from the pan and set it aside in a warm place. Add the artichokes to the pan and cook for 20 minutes.

Return the meat to the pan and cook for another 5 minutes.

Meanwhile, beat the eggs and lemon juice in a large bowl. Add the chopped parsley and season with a pinch of salt. When the lamb is cooked, quickly add the egg mixture to the meat, stir for a few seconds, then remove the pan from the heat. The eggs must not coagulate but lightly coat the pieces of meat. Transfer everything to a serving dish and serve.

Ricotta waffles

Ferratelle con la ricotta

Ferratelle are waffle-style cookies, named for the iron plates used to make them—similar to a waffle iron. These were traditionally served as a snack to guests at country wedding celebrations.

PREPARATION TIME 45 minutes
COOKING TIME 1 hour
SERVES 6–8

7 fl oz/scant 1 cup/200 ml oil, plus extra for greasing
1 pound 2 ounces/generous 4 cups/500 g all-purpose (plain) flour
1 teaspoon baking powder
5 eggs, beaten
9 ounces/generous 1 cup/250 g superfine (caster) sugar
1 teaspoon vanilla extract
Few drops of lemon juice
Mixed berries, to serve
Whipped cream, to serve

FOR THE FILLING
1 pound 2 ounces/2¼ cups/500 g ewe's milk ricotta cheese
7 ounces/generous ¾ cup/200 g superfine (caster) sugar
3½ fl oz/scant ½ cup/100 ml Aurum orange liqueur

Lightly grease a ferratella iron with oil.

Sift the flour and baking powder together into a large bowl. Add the beaten eggs, sugar, vanilla extract, lemon juice, and oil and mix well to combine. Spread 1 tablespoon of the batter on the lightly greased surface of the ferratella iron, set it on the heat, and cook the waffle on both sides. Remove and repeat until all the batter is used up.

To make the filling, mix the ricotta, sugar, and liqueur together in a large bowl until creamy. Place a small amount of filling on the waffles and fold them over as if making ravioli. Arrange the ferratelle in a serving dish and serve them with berries and whipped cream alongside.

Chocolate-covered spiced cookies

Originally made with cooked grape must (mosto cotto) and called mostaccioli, these diamond-shaped, chocolate-covered spiced cookies date back to Roman times, and are traditionally served at Christmas.

PREPARATION TIME 10 minutes

COOKING TIME 1 hour

RESTING TIME 1 hour

SERVES 8

1 pound 5 ounces/2⅔ cups/600 g honey

10½ ounces/1⅓ cups/300 g superfine (caster) sugar

2 tablespoons unsweetened cocoa powder

7 ounces/1½ cups/200 g blanched almonds, toasted and chopped

Grated zest of 2 oranges

1 teaspoon ground cinnamon

5 ounces/1¼ cups/150 g all-purpose (plain) flour, plus extra for dusting

Unsalted butter, for greasing

FOR THE FROSTING (ICING)

1 ounce/¼ stick/30 g unsalted butter

1 pound 2 ounces/500 g dark chocolate

Put the honey into a saucepan, ideally copper, set it over a medium heat, and add the sugar and cocoa powder while stirring continuously with a wooden spoon. When the sugar melts, carefully mix in the almonds, orange zest, and cinnamon and cook for a few minutes, then remove from the heat and set aside to cool.

Sift the flour into a large bowl. Once the honey mixture is cool, incorporate enough flour into the mixture to form a dough. Transfer to a clean work surface and knead until the dough is smooth and soft, then cover with plastic wrap (cling film) and leave it to rest for 1 hour.

Preheat the oven to 325 °F/160 °C/140 °C Fan/Gas 3. Grease a large baking sheet with butter and add a dusting of flour.

Using a rolling pin, roll out the dough to a ¾-inch/2-cm thickness. Cut it lengthwise into 1¼-inch/3-cm wide strips then crosswise into diamond-shaped cookies (biscuits). Place the cookies on the prepared baking sheet and bake in the preheated oven for about 30 minutes. Remove from the oven and leave to cool.

To make the frosting (icing), add the butter and chopped chocolate to a heatproof bowl, set over a saucepan of simmering water, making sure the bottom of the bowl doesn't touch the water, and leave to melt. Dip one cookie at a time into the chocolate mixture, then drain and place on a cooling rack to dry and turn glossy.

Arrange the cookies on a serving plate and serve.

Campania

Exquisite foods to make you sing

Campania is said to be a land whose flavors delight the palate just as Mother Nature
made them. Tons of fragrant vegetables flood the markets where green friarielli
(broccoli rabe, with their wonderfully bitter taste) are in great demand, where
eggplants (aubergines) seem specially designed to be made into timbales, where
lemons from the Amalfi Coast become the most elegant of salads or are bottled as
delicious limoncello to be sipped while admiring the sunset on the sea. It is where San
Marzano tomatoes reign supreme and leavened doughs or spaghetti serve as a soft
pillow. It is where someone in the Cilento region invented the wonder that is
mozzarella by processing the milk of the buffaloes that were brought here from Asia
centuries ago. Naked and raw, mozzarella melts in the mouth; when served with
tomatoes, it is in the Caprese style (page 241); and, anywhere in the world, there can
be no pizza (page 238) without it. Campania is still a region of deep-rooted traditions,
which is why the sweet side of life is celebrated with pastries, such as custard-filled
sfogliatelle and babas (page 248) of legendary lightness.

Pizza Margherita

Making your own pizza is an undeniable pleasure, and this recipe doesn't require too much time, yet the result is a puffy crust, crispy surface, and a soft yet cooked through topping.

PREPARATION TIME 20 minutes
COOKING TIME 15 minutes
RISING TIME 1 hour
MAKES 2

½ ounce/15 g fresh yeast
About 3½ fl oz/scant ½ cup/100 ml lukewarm water
9 ounces/2 cups/250 g Italian "00" or "0" flour
Extra-virgin olive oil, for greasing and drizzling
Salt

FOR THE TOPPING
2 pounds 4 ounces/1 kg ripe tomatoes, skinned, seeded, and cut
  into small pieces
9–10½ ounces/250–300 g mozzarella cheese, sliced and drained
Basil leaves
Salt

To make the pizza dough, place the yeast in a cup and stir in a little of the lukewarm water. Sift the flour into a bowl, then mix 2 ounces/50 g of the flour into the yeast mixture to form a starter, adding more water as necessary. Leave to rise for 15 minutes.

Gather the remaining flour into a mound on a work surface. Add a pinch of salt and make a well in the center. Add the prepared starter to the well and knead the mixture energetically, adding as much lukewarm water as needed to form a soft dough. Leave the dough to rise until it has doubled in volume.

Divide the dough in half and roll out each half into a disk. Grease two round baking sheets, about 8–9½ inches/20–24 cm in diameter, well with oil and line

them with the dough. Cover with a dish (tea) towel and leave to prove for 15 minutes.

For the sauce, leave the tomato pieces to drain in a strainer (sieve).

When the dough has risen, preheat the oven to 480 °F/250 °C/230 °C Fan/Gas 10.

Spread the tomatoes over the top of the pizza dough, leaving ½ inch/1 cm free around the edges. Season with salt, drizzle with a little oil, and bake in the preheated oven for about 10 minutes. Remove the pizzas from the oven, dot the top with the mozzarella and basil, drizzle with oil, and return to the oven for about 5 minutes. The pizza is ready when the crust is well browned.

Eggplant Parmigiana

Melanzane alla Parmigiana

There are so many variations of this much-loved classic, but tradition dictates that the eggplants (aubergines) must be fried (not grilled) before baking. The dish only improves if served a day after it is made.

PREPARATION TIME 45 minutes
COOKING TIME 50 minutes
RESTING TIME 3 hours
SERVES 6

2 pounds 12 ounces/1.2 kg eggplants (aubergines), cut lengthwise into slices ¼ inch/5 mm thick
2–3 tablespoons extra-virgin olive oil
½ onion, chopped
1 clove garlic, unpeeled and lightly crushed
17 fl oz/2 cups/500 ml puréed strained tomatoes (passata)
1 bunch basil, leaves picked
½ teaspoon sugar (optional)
All-purpose (plain) flour, for coating
34 fl oz/4¼ cups/1 liter vegetable oil, for frying
3½ ounces/1¼ cups/100 g grated Parmesan cheese
10½ ounces/300 g mozzarella cheese, sliced
Salt and black pepper

Place the eggplant (aubergine) slices in a colander, sprinkle with salt, and leave for about 1 hour to expel their excess moisture. Rinse, drain, and squeeze dry.

Heat the extra-virgin olive oil in a large saucepan, add the onion and garlic, and sauté for a few minutes. Remove and discard the garlic and add the puréed strained tomatoes (passata) and half the basil. Season with salt, pepper, and the sugar, if using, and cook for 15–20 minutes.

Spread the flour out on a large plate and toss the eggplants in the flour until coated. Heat the oil for frying in a large, deep pan, add the eggplants, a few at a time, and fry until golden on both sides. Remove from the pan with a slotted spoon and drain on paper towels.

To assemble the dish, spread some of the tomato sauce over the bottom of an ovenproof dish, then arrange a layer of fried eggplant on top. Cover with a few tablespoons of grated Parmesan, a few basil leaves, and the mozzarella slices. Continue to make layers in the same order until all the ingredients are used up. Ideally, if you have time, set it aside to cool and firm up for 2 hours before cooking.

Preheat the oven to 350 °F/180 °C/160 °C Fan/Gas 4.

Bake in the preheated oven for 30 minutes, or until the top is golden and bubbling. Remove from the oven and leave to rest at room temperature before serving.

Caprese salad with buffalo mozzarella

Caprese di
mozzarella di bufala

A classic, simple antipasto dish of the finest ingredients:
sliced tomatoes, buffalo mozzarella, and basil leaves.
The colors of the dish are famously said to replicate
the Italian flag.

PREPARATION TIME 20 minutes

SERVES 4

3–4 tomatoes
1 × 10½-ounce/300-g ball buffalo mozzarella
Handful of basil leaves
Extra-virgin olive oil, for drizzling
Salt

Wash, skin, slice, and deseed the tomatoes. Cut the
mozzarella into 2–3-mm slices.

Arrange alternating tomato and cheese slices into
concentric circles on a serving dish.

Sprinkle with fresh basil leaves, drizzle with oil and
season with salt. Refrigerate until ready to serve.

Rice timbale

One of the most iconic Neapolitan dishes, this is not an everyday dish, but one for special occasions, as you need to allow time to prepare and cook the various elements of this extraordinary creation.

PREPARATION TIME 2 hours
COOKING TIME 2 hours 30 minutes
SOAKING TIME 1 hour
SERVES 12

FOR THE MEAT SAUCE
2–3 tablespoons tomato paste (purée)
1 onion, chopped
2 celery stalks, chopped
2 carrots, chopped
3½ ounces/100 g cured ham
4 tablespoons olive oil
1 pound 5 ounces/2⅔ cups/600 g ground (minced) veal
3½ fl oz/scant ½ cup/100 ml dry white wine
Meat stock, for cooking
Salt and black pepper

FOR THE MEATBALLS
1 slice white sandwich bread
3½ ounces/scant ½ cup/100 g ground (minced) veal
1 egg yolk
½ teaspoon chopped parsley
Olive oil, for cooking

FOR THE RISOTTO
2 ounces/3½ tablespoons/50 g unsalted butter
1 pound 10 ounces/4¼ cups/750 g Arborio or Carnaroli rice
85 fl oz/10 cups/2.5 liters lukewarm chicken stock
3 ounces/1 cup/80 g grated Parmesan cheese
3 eggs

TO ASSEMBLE
¾ cup/20 g dried mushrooms
1 tablespoon unsalted butter, plus extra for the top
2 ounces/50 g cooked ham, chopped
5½ ounces/150 g Italian sausage, removed from casing and crumbled
2 hard-boiled eggs, chopped
5½ ounces/150 g mozzarella cheese, diced
7 ounces/1⅔ cups/200 g peas
3 ounces/80 g Parmesan cheese
Bread crumbs, for sprinkling

Soak the dried mushrooms for the assembly in a bowl of hot water for 1 hour. Drain and set aside.

For the meat sauce, in a small bowl, dilute the tomato paste (purée) with a little water. Place the onion, celery, carrots, ham, and oil in a large saucepan with a lid (preferably a terracotta cooking pot) and cook over a low heat for 2–3 minutes. Increase the heat, add the ground (minced) veal, and stir until it is browned all over.

Pour in the wine and stir to scrape up all the crispy bits off the bottom of the pan, then allow it to evaporate. Add the diluted tomato paste and season with salt and pepper. Pour in enough stock to cover the contents of the pan, cover with a lid, and simmer for 1 hour, adding more stock if necessary.

To make the meatballs, place the bread in a bowl, cover with water, and leave to soak until it has absorbed the water, then squeeze out the liquid. Add the soaked bread to a large bowl with the ground (minced) veal, egg yolk, and parsley and mix together. Season with salt. Using your hands, shape a little of the mixture at a time into hazelnut-size balls. Heat a little oil in a large skillet (frying pan), add the meatballs in batches if necessary, and fry them until they are browned all over. Set aside.

For the risotto, melt half the butter in a large pan, add the rice, and cook for 10–12 minutes, gradually adding a little of the lukewarm stock at a time until it is absorbed. Remove from the heat and set aside to cool. Add the remaining butter, the cheese, and the eggs and mix to combine. Season with salt and pepper.

Preheat the oven to 400 °F/200 °C/180 °C Fan/Gas 6.

Melt the butter in a small skillet (frying pan), add the soaked mushrooms and ham, and cook for a few minutes. Remove from the pan and set aside. Add the crumbled sausage and fry for a few minutes, then set aside.

Set aside a little of the risotto, then line the bottom and sides of a 10½-inch/26-cm round cake pan (tin) or oven-proof dish with the remainder, pressing so that the rice sticks well. Fill the pan with the chopped eggs, mozzarella, peas, mushrooms and ham, the sausage, meatballs, and Parmesan, alternating with tablespoons of the meat sauce.

Cover with the remaining risotto and sprinkle with bread crumbs and small butter curls. Cover well with parchment paper or aluminum foil and bake in the preheated oven for 1 hour. Close to the end of the cooking time, uncover to allow the top to turn golden. Remove from the oven and leave to rest for 15 minutes, then turn it out. Serve with the remaining meat sauce.

Bread-crumbed mussels

Another popular, classic antipasto dish of the region: the tender mussels are covered in a crispy, flavorful golden crust, oven-baked, and eaten straight from the shell.

PREPARATION TIME 45 minutes

COOKING TIME 10–15 minutes

SERVES 6

3 pounds/1.5 kg mussels, cleaned (page 323)
9 ounces/5 cups/250 g bread crumbs
2 tablespoons chopped parsley
2 cloves garlic, chopped
1 ounce/30 g capers
3½ fl oz/scant ½ cup/100 ml extra-virgin olive oil
Salt and black pepper

Preheat the oven to 375 °F/190 °C/170 °C Fan/Gas 5. Line a large baking sheet with parchment paper, and line a fine-mesh strainer (sieve) with cheesecloth (muslin) and set aside.

Put the mussels into a large saucepan, cover with a lid, and place over a high heat for 6–8 minutes until they open. Drain immediately, collecting their liquor in a bowl, then strain the liquor through the lined strainer. Discard the empty half-shells and place the mussels in their shells on the prepared baking sheet. Discard any mussels that remain closed.

Combine the bread crumbs with the chopped parsley, garlic, and capers in a large bowl. Season with salt and pepper and add the oil. Stir well and add a little of the reserved liquor to lightly moisten the mixture (take care not to let it become too wet and soggy).

Using a teaspoon, spread the mixture over each mussel, covering it well. Cook the mussels in the oven for 5 minutes. Given the quantities in this recipe, you will need to cook them in several batches. Remove from the oven and serve hot or lukewarm.

Ischia-style rabbit

Ischia is known for its abundance of wild rabbits, and every local family has a slightly different method of preparing this iconic Sunday lunch dish, handed down the generations, and still ubiquitous today.

PREPARATION TIME 20 minutes

COOKING TIME 50 minutes

MARINATING TIME 2 hours

SERVES 4–5

3 pounds 5 ounces/1.5 kg rabbit pieces

8 fl oz/1 cup/250 ml white wine

7 fl oz/scant 1 cup/200 ml extra-virgin olive oil

4 cloves garlic, unpeeled and lightly crushed

15 Pizzutello cherry tomatoes, halved or quartered depending on size

Handful of basil leaves

Salt and black pepper

Place the rabbit pieces in a large bowl, pour in the wine, cover with plastic wrap (cling film), and leave to marinate in the refrigerator for about 2 hours.

Heat the oil in a large saucepan with a lid over a high heat, add the garlic, and sauté for a few minutes, then remove and discard the garlic. Drain the rabbit pieces, setting aside the marinade, then add the rabbit to the pan and brown each piece evenly. Pour in half the marinade and stir to scrape up all the crispy bits off the bottom of the pan, then allow it to evaporate.

Add the tomatoes to the pan, season lightly with salt and pepper, and mix well. Cover with a lid, and cook over a medium-low heat for 30–40 minutes. Check frequently, adding a little hot water occasionally, if necessary, to prevent the meat from drying out.

When cooked, add a handful of basil leaves. Leave to rest for a few minutes before serving.

Neapolitan cheesecake

The most famous version of this delicious cheesecake-style pie is this one from Naples. Authentic pastiera is made with a jarred grain—grano cotto—but you can use wheat berries or pearl barley instead.

PREPARATION TIME 2 hours

COOKING TIME 1 hour 30 minutes

RESTING TIME 12 hours

SERVES 8–10

6 ounces/1½ sticks/175 g unsalted butter or lard

5 ounces/scant ⅔ cup/140 g superfine (caster) sugar

2 eggs

Grated zest of 1 orange

12 ounces/scant 3 cups/350 g all-purpose (plain) flour, plus extra for dusting

FOR THE FILLING

10½ ounces/2¼ cups/300 g precooked wheat berries (grains)

7 fl oz/scant 1 cup/200 ml milk

Grated zest of 2 oranges

9 ounces/generous 1 cup/250 g superfine (caster) sugar

12 ounces/1¾ cups/350 g ricotta cheese

2 eggs

1 egg yolk

Pinch of salt

Grated zest of 1 lemon

5½ ounces/generous 1 cup/150 g candied fruit (citron and orange), cut into small cubes

2 teaspoons orange flower water

For the filling, place the wheat berries in a large saucepan with the milk, grated zest of 1 orange, and 1 tablespoon of the sugar and cook, stirring continuously until the milk is completely absorbed. Remove from the heat and set aside to cool.

In a large bowl, mix the ricotta with the remaining sugar until smooth and soft. Add the eggs, egg yolk, salt, and the grated zest of the remaining orange and all the lemon zest. Stir with a wooden spoon, then add the candied fruit and the orange flower water. Finally, add the cold wheat berry mixture and mix until smooth. Refrigerate.

Meanwhile, to make the dough, place the butter and sugar in a large bowl and mix together, then incorporate

the eggs, orange zest, and flour. Mix and knead until a compact dough forms, then wrap it in plastic wrap (cling film) and refrigerate until cold.

Preheat the oven to 350 °F/180 °C/160 °C Fan/Gas 4.

Roll out two-thirds of the dough on a lightly floured work surface and use it to line a 12-inch/30-cm nonstick baking pan (tin). Add the filling, then roll out the remaining dough and cut it into strips. Decorate the top of the pie by arranging the strips into a diamond lattice. Bake in the preheated oven for about 1 hour 20 minutes. Remove from the oven and set aside to cool at room temperature or in the refrigerator for 12 hours before serving.

Rum baba

Rhum baba

⊚ p. 250

This mushroom-shaped, rum-soaked cake is one of Campania's finest treats, found in every *pasticceria*. The dessert originated in France, making its way to Naples, via chefs of the royal family, in the 1800s.

PREPARATION TIME 1 hour 30 minutes
COOKING TIME 55 minutes
RISING TIME 2 hours 30 minutes
SERVES 8

FOR THE FRUIT
4–5 tablespoons currants
8 ripe plums, halved and pitted
3½ fl oz/scant ½ cup /100 ml rum
2 apples, peeled and cut into 8 segments
3 pears, peeled and cut into 6 segments
3 tablespoons superfine (caster) sugar
Grated zest of ½ lemon
2 walnuts, chopped
4 lightly toasted almonds, chopped

FOR THE BABAS
¾ ounce/25 g fresh yeast
2 tablespoons superfine (caster) sugar
1¾ fl oz/scant ¼ cup/50 ml lukewarm milk
4½ ounces/1⅛ sticks/125 g unsalted butter, softened, plus extra
  for greasing
9 ounces/2 cups/250 g all-purpose (plain) flour, plus extra
  for dusting
3 eggs, beaten
Salt

FOR THE SYRUP
1 pound/2 cups/450 g superfine (caster) sugar
10 fl oz/1¼ cups/300 ml rum
1¾ fl oz/scant ¼ cup/50 ml lemon juice
Grated zest of ½ lemon

FOR THE GLAZE
2 tablespoons apricot jam
2 tablespoons rum

→ CAMPANIA

248

To prepare the fruit, put the currants and plums into a large bowl, cover them with the rum and leave to soak until soft. Drain and squeeze over a bowl, setting the rum aside.

Place the apples, pears, sugar, currants, and plums in a large saucepan. Add the lemon zest, 3½ fl oz/scant ½ cup/100 ml water, and reserved rum and cook for about 10 minutes. Add the walnuts and almonds, stir, and cook for another 10 minutes, then remove from the heat and set aside.

To make the babas, add the yeast to a cup with a pinch of the sugar and a little of the milk and stir until the yeast and sugar have dissolved. Leave to stand for 10 minutes.

Grease a large bowl with butter. Gather the flour into a mound on a clean work surface and make a well in the center. Add a pinch of salt, the yeast mixture, the remaining sugar, half the softened butter, and half the beaten eggs to the well. Pour in the remaining milk and mix everything together while working vigorously to a dough. Add the remaining eggs and butter and knead until the dough comes away from the work surface. Transfer the dough to the prepared bowl, cover with plastic wrap (cling film), and leave to rise in a warm place for about 1 hour 30 minutes.

Grease eight baba molds with butter and add a dusting of flour. Alternatively, use a 2.6–3.2-quart/2.5–3-liter donut mold. As the dough is very soft, use a wooden spoon to carefully fill the baba molds. Cover and leave to prove until the dough reaches the rim.

Preheat the oven to 375 °F/190 °C/170 °C Fan/Gas 5.

Bake the babas in the preheated oven for 15 minutes, then reduce the oven temperature to 325 °F/170 °C/150 °C Fan/Gas 3 and bake for another 15–20 minutes.

Meanwhile, make the syrup by boiling 15 fl oz/generous 1⅔ cups/450 ml water and the sugar together in a pan for 5 minutes. Remove from the heat and wait for a few minutes before adding the rum, lemon juice, and zest.

Turn out the babas, leave to rest for 5 minutes, then return them to the molds. Prick them all over with a toothpick (cocktail stick) and slowly moisten them with a little hot syrup, waiting until it has been well absorbed before adding more syrup. The babas should absorb almost the entire batch of syrup.

When it is time to serve, for the glaze, stir the jam and rum together in a small bowl until combined. Turn the babas out on a serving plate and brush them with a thin layer of the glaze. Decorate with the cooked fruit. Serve the babas at the table with more syrup.

Lemon delights

p. 251

Delicious individual cakes traditionally made on the Sorrentine Peninsula for special occasions. Invented by the pastry chef Carmine Marzuillo in 1978, they became a symbol of Campania's pastry tradition.

PREPARATION TIME 3 hours
COOKING TIME 40 minutes
CHILLING TIME 10 hours
MAKES 7–8

FOR THE SPONGE BASE
Unsalted butter, for greasing
3½ ounces/generous ¾ cup/100 g "00" flour,
  plus extra for dusting
5 ounces/150 g eggs, at room temperature
5 ounces/⅔ cup/150 g granulated sugar
½ vanilla bean (pod), split in half lengthwise and seeds
  scraped out
2 ounces/50 g potato starch (*fecola di patate*)

FOR THE LEMON CREAM
Grated zest of 1 lemon
3 tablespoons lemon juice
2 egg yolks
1½ ounces/scant ¼ cup/40 g superfine (caster) sugar
3 tablespoons unsalted butter, diced

FOR THE PASTRY CREAM
4 egg yolks
3½ ounces/scant ½ cup/100 g superfine (caster) sugar
1 ounce/¼ cup/30 g all-purpose (plain) flour
17 fl oz/2 cups/500 ml milk
1 teaspoon vanilla extract or grated lemon zest

FOR THE LIMONCELLO SYRUP
1 ounce/generous ⅛ cup/30 g superfine (caster) sugar
Grated zest of ½ lemon
1¾ fl oz/scant ¼ cup/50 ml limoncello

FOR THE FILLING
2 tablespoons whipped cream
2 tablespoons limoncello

FOR THE FROSTING (ICING)
2¾ fl oz/⅓ cup/80 ml whipped cream
2 tablespoons milk
Whipped cream or grated lemon zest, to decorate

Preheat the oven to 325 °F/170 °C/150 °C Fan/Gas 3. Grease eight aluminum hemispherical mini cake pans (tins) with butter and add a dusting of flour (omit this step if using silicone molds).

For the sponge cake batter, whisk the eggs, granulated sugar, and vanilla seeds in a stand mixer fitted with a whisk attachment, or in a bowl with an electric whisk at medium speed, until it is a light, foamy mixture. Sift the flour into a large bowl with the potato starch, then gently mix into the egg mixture with a spatula until combined. Spoon the cake batter into the prepared pans until the batter comes ¼ inch/5 mm below the rims. Bake for 15 minutes. Remove from the oven and set aside to cool, then turn the sponge domes out onto a large plate. Cover with plastic wrap (cling film) and set aside.

To make the lemon cream, place the lemon zest in a bowl and add the juice. Leave to steep for 5–10 minutes. In another bowl, beat the egg yolks with the superfine sugar until fluffy, then add the lemon zest and juice. Transfer to a saucepan and stir continuously while heating gently, taking care not to bring it to a boil. Leave to cool, then add the diced butter. Using a handheld blender, blend the cream until smooth, then cover with plastic wrap and refrigerate.

To make the pastry cream, beat the egg yolks and superfine sugar together in a medium bowl with a wooden spoon. Add the flour, a little at a time, stirring until the mixture is combined.

Heat the milk in a saucepan with the vanilla extract or grated lemon zest, then gradually whisk the milk into the egg yolks. Place over the heat and simmer for 3–4 minutes, stirring continuously. Do not exceed

180 °F/82 °C in temperature. The correct temperature is 183–185 °F/84–85 °C, but it is advisable not to exceed 180 °F/82 °C, because the cream will continue to cook even once the pan is removed from the heat.

Pour the cream into a bowl and let it cool by stirring it occasionally (or cover with plastic wrap so that the wrap does not touch the surface). Once it's cool, refrigerate.

Make the limoncello syrup by bringing 1 fl oz/ 2 tablespoons/30 ml water, the sugar, and lemon zest to a boil in a saucepan. Remove from the heat and stir in the limoncello. Set aside until cool.

To fill the sponge domes, make an incision in the flat bottom of each dome and carefully hollow it out, setting aside the sponge. In a bowl, mix half of the lemon cream with half of the pastry cream, then add the whipped cream and limoncello. Mix well and carefully fill the domes. Cover the hole in the bottom of the domes using the previously removed sponge.

Turn the domes over and prick them with a toothpick (cocktail stick) in several places. Using a brush, soak them in the limoncello syrup and set aside.

In another bowl, make the frosting (icing) by mixing the remaining lemon cream and pastry cream, the whipped cream, and milk together in a large bowl.

Arrange the lemon delights on a serving plate and cover them with plenty of frosting. Refrigerate for at least 8–10 hours before serving. Decorate with a spoonful of whipped cream or lemon zest.

Basilicata

Bread, pasta, and ... chile

In the Basilicata region, food traditions are still respected, both out of duty and pleasure. Chile pepper is sprinkled liberally over everything. Appetizers (starters) see pasta combined with vegetables, legumes (pulses), and grains: the Lucani, as the inhabitants are known, are epicureans and proud of their lagane with chickpeas (page 259). And the region's artisan aged, semi-mature, and fresh cheeses are pure pleasure for the palate, including braided mozzarella and bocconcini, burrini, provole, scamorze, savory caciocavallo podolico, ewe's milk and goat's milk pecorino, and three varieties of ricotta classified by type of flavor and seasoning—from fresh to soft and sweet, to strong, spicier, and more compact for grating. As always, there is a mouthwatering variety of excellent cured meats with a healthy, strong taste, such as the ancient lucanica, a sausage known since Roman times. Then there is the calming scent of bread: the bread from Matera is considered by many to be the best in Italy. And, finally, the vineyards on the slopes of Mount Vulture smell wonderfully of Aglianico grapes. As for nature in Basilicata, you just have to imagine the enchantment of the Pollino National Park, where you can admire the sun as it rises over the Ionian Sea and sets over the Tyrrhenian Sea.

Fusilli with bread crumbs

Originally a peasant dish from the Basilicata region, this uses simple and inexpensive ingredients—stale bread, anchovies, garlic, and chili—to great effect, in a first course that can be ready in minutes.

PREPARATION TIME 10 minutes

COOKING TIME 25 minutes

SOAKING TIME 5–20 minutes

SERVES 4

4 salt-packed anchovy fillets
2 tablespoons extra-virgin olive oil
1 small piece of dried chile or pinch of chili flakes
3½ ounces/100 g stale bread, processed into crumbs
12 ounces/350 g fusilli
2 ounces/scant ⅔ cup/50 g grated pecorino cheese
2 tablespoons chopped parsley
Salt

Soak the anchovies in a bowl of water for 5–20 minutes, then drain and set aside.

Heat the oil in a skillet (frying pan), add the dried chile, anchovies, and bread crumbs, and stir until the anchovies are almost completely dissolved.

Cook the pasta in a large saucepan of salted water for 10 minutes, or until al dente. Drain, reserving a ladleful of the cooking water, then add the pasta to the pan with the chile and bread crumbs. Sprinkle with the grated cheese, then toss the pasta over a high heat for a few minutes, adding 1 tablespoon of the reserved pasta cooking water, if necessary.

Sprinkle with chopped parsley and serve straight from the pan.

Lagane with chickpeas

Wide, ribbon-like lagane is believed to be the oldest pasta—the first known reference to this dish was by the poet Horace in the first century B.C. in his home town of Venosa.

PREPARATION TIME 30 minutes
COOKING TIME 2 hours 40 minutes
SOAKING TIME 12 hours
SERVES 4

9 ounces/1½ cups/250 g dried chickpeas
1 bay leaf
2–3 tablespoons olive oil, plus extra for drizzling
1 clove garlic, peeled and left whole
Pinch of chili powder
7 ounces/1¼ cups/200 g chopped tomatoes
14 ounces/400 g lagane
Salt and black pepper

Soak the chickpeas in a large bowl of water for 12 hours, then drain.

Place the chickpeas and bay leaf in a large saucepan, cover with plenty of water, and cook for 2 hours, or until the chickpeas are tender. Drain, discarding the bay leaf, and set aside.

Heat the oil in a large skillet (frying pan), add the garlic, and sauté until colored, then remove from the pan and discard. Add the chili powder and tomatoes, season with salt and pepper, and cook over a medium heat for 10 minutes. Add the chickpeas and sauté for another 10 minutes.

Meanwhile, cook the pasta in a large saucepan of salted water for 10 minutes, or until al dente. Drain the pasta and add to the pan with the sauce. Toss the pasta in the sauce to flavor, season with salt and pepper, and drizzle with oil. Serve immediately.

Horseradish omelet

Rafanata

This uniquely traditional dish from Basilicata
is essentially a horseradish omelet—the name
originates from *rafano*, the horseradish root,
known in Basilicata as "the poor man's truffle."

PREPARATION TIME 15 minutes

COOKING TIME 20–30 minutes

SERVES 4–6

12 ounces/350 g potatoes, unpeeled
5 eggs
3½ ounces/generous ¾ cup/100 g grated pecorino cheese
3½ ounces/100 g horseradish, peeled and finely grated
Extra-virgin olive oil, for cooking
Salt and black pepper

Cook the potatoes in a large saucepan of boiling water
until soft. Using a slotted spoon, remove the potatoes
from the pan and, while still hot, mash them with a
potato ricer into a bowl. Set aside to cool.

Mix the eggs, cheese, and horseradish together in
a large bowl. Season with salt and pepper and whisk
until smooth. Add the mixture to the cooled potatoes
and mix with a spoon to combine.

Heat a few tablespoons of oil in a large skillet (frying
pan) with a lid over a high heat. Add the omelet mixture
and spread it over the pan with a spoon. Cook for
2–3 minutes, then reduce the heat, cover, and cook
for another 10 minutes. Check that the omelet has set
enough for it to be turned. Using the lid, turn it over and
cook it for a few minutes on the other side until golden.

Transfer to a serving dish, cut it into slices, and serve
hot or cold.

Salt cod with crusco peppers

Crusco peppers are a familiar summer sight throughout Basilicata, the brilliant red garlands of peppers hanging from houses to dry in a traditional process that gives them their flavor and crunch.

PREPARATION TIME 30 minutes

COOKING TIME 15 minutes

SOAKING TIME 24 hours

SERVES 4

1 pound 9 ounces/700 g salt cod, rinsed

1¾ fl oz/scant ¼ cup/50 ml olive oil

7 ounces/200 g dried crusco peppers, cut into small pieces and seeded

2 tablespoons finely chopped parsley

Soak the salt cod in a large bowl of water in the refrigerator for at least 24 hours, changing the water several times. Drain.

Put the cod into a large saucepan filled with cold water and set it over a medium heat. When the water comes to a simmer, cover the pan with a lid, reduce the heat, and simmer gently for 8 minutes (any longer and the flesh will become fibrous). Drain and cut the fish into several medium-sized pieces. Remove any bones, slice, and arrange it in a serving dish.

Heat the oil in a medium skillet (frying pan). Remove the pan from the heat and add the dried peppers. The heat of the oil will soon make them crispy. Pour the oil with the peppers over the cod, sprinkle with finely chopped parsley, and serve.

Fava bean purée with wild chicory

Purée di fave e cicorielle

A dish of the *cucina povera* tradition, the soft and delicate white bean purée is complemented by the tender, slightly bitter wild chicory. Serve with toasted bread and a good extra-virgin olive oil.

PREPARATION TIME 25 minutes

COOKING TIME 3 hours 30 minutes

SOAKING TIME 12 hours

SERVES 6

2 pounds 4 ounces/1 kg dried fava (broad) beans
6 pounds 8 ounces/3 kg wild chicory
2 tablespoons extra virgin olive oil, plus extra for drizzling
1 clove garlic, peeled and left whole
1 onion, chopped
1 celery stalk, chopped
2 tomatoes, skinned and seeded
½ bunch parsley, chopped
Salt and black pepper

Soak the fava (broad) beans in a large bowl of water for 12 hours.

The next day, drain the beans, peel, and cook them in a large saucepan of water over a low heat for 3 hours, or until tender. Purée the beans by pushing them through a strainer (sieve) into a bowl and set aside.

Cook the chicory in a large saucepan of boiling salted water for 10–15 minutes, then drain and coarsely chop the leaves. Heat the oil in a large skillet (frying pan), add the garlic, and sauté until colored, then remove and discard the garlic. Add the chicory and sauté it for a few minutes. Heat the fava bean purée in a separate pan, adjust the seasoning with salt, then add the vegetables, drizzle with oil, and serve with black pepper.

Rionero-style pork stew

The recipe takes its name from the town of Rionero, located in the north of Basilicata. This light stew, flavored with garlic and chile, cooks at an almost imperceptible simmer, described locally as *pipitiare*.

PREPARATION TIME 10 minutes

COOKING TIME 2 hours 30 minutes

RESTING TIME 1 hour

SERVES 6

2 pounds 4 ounces/1 kg lean pork
3 fl oz/scant ½ cup/100 ml oil
2 cloves garlic, peeled and left whole
1 tablespoon lard (optional)
7–10 fl oz/scant 1–1¼ cups/200–300 ml white wine vinegar
3 onions, thinly sliced
1 red chile, thinly sliced
Salt and black pepper

Rub the meat with 3 tablespoons of the oil and one of the garlic cloves, then leave to stand for 1 hour. Cut it into pieces.

Heat the remaining oil in a large saucepan with a lid (preferably a terracotta cooking pot) together with the lard, if desired. Add the remaining garlic clove and sauté for a few minutes, then remove and discard it. Add the meat to the pan and brown it well, then add enough vinegar to cover the contents of the pan and allow it to evaporate.

Add the onions and enough of the chile according to taste and season with salt and pepper. Cover the pan with parchment paper, then cover it tightly with the lid and cook for 2 hours over a very low heat.

Chestnut turnovers

Deep-fried pastries filled with chickpeas, chestnuts, and chocolate are a Christmas specialty of the region. The chestnut harvest is celebrated at a festival every October in the hillside village of Trecchina.

PREPARATION TIME 45 minutes

COOKING TIME 2 hours 15 minutes

SOAKING TIME 12 hours

RESTING TIME 10 minutes

SERVES 8

2 pounds 4 ounces/8⅓ cups/1 kg all-purpose (plain) flour, plus extra for dusting
10½ ounces/1⅓ cups/300 g superfine (caster) sugar
7 eggs
4 fl oz/½ cup/120 ml sweet white wine
10½ ounces/2¾ sticks/300 g unsalted butter
Vegetable oil, for deep-frying
Honey, for drizzling

FOR THE FILLING
7 ounces/1¼ cups/200 g dried chickpeas
2 pounds 4 ounces/scant 7½ cups/1 kg chestnuts
3½ ounces/1 cup/100 g unsweetened cocoa powder
Anise, to taste
Superfine (caster) sugar, to taste

For the filling, soak the chickpeas in a large bowl of water for 12 hours, then drain.

Cook the chickpeas in a large saucepan of water for 2 hours, or until tender. Drain. Meanwhile, cook the chestnuts in another pan of water for 20 minutes, or until tender. Drain and add them to a food processor with the chickpeas and blitz until smooth. Transfer to a bowl, add the cocoa and the desired amount of anise and sugar, and mix until combined. Set aside.

Gather the flour in a mound on a clean work surface and make a well in the center. Add the sugar to the well, followed by the eggs and wine, and knead to a smooth and compact dough. Gather the dough into a ball, cover, and leave to rest at room temperature for 10 minutes.

Roll out the dough on a lightly floured work surface and cut out lots of squares. Place a little of the chickpea and chestnut filling into the center of half of the squares, then cover with a second square to enclose the filling. Seal the edges by crimping with the tines of a fork. You could also shape the dough into half-moons by cutting out circles of dough instead.

Heat enough oil for deep-frying in a large, deep saucepan to 350 °F/180 °C on a thermometer, or until a cube of bread browns in 30 seconds. Carefully add the turnovers to the oil and deep-fry until golden. Remove with a slotted spoon and drain on paper towels. Arrange them in a serving dish and drizzle with honey.

Puglia

Where oil is truly liquid gold

Tens of thousands of olive trees. In Puglia, nature has sown wondrous seeds, and those mighty trees bear abundant olives that over the years have produced oils of excellent quality with distinct characteristics. Those oils impart their goodness to a simple cuisine, with flavors little changed, that draws from a wealth of vegetable gardens so bountiful that they supply markets all over Italy. For instance, fava (broad) beans—whether fresh, raw, cooked, or dried—are practically a daily staple, and macco, a tasty purée made from them is among the most delicious dishes one can try. Still very much in vogue are other time-honored dishes, such as the famous orecchiette pasta with cime di rapa (broccoli rabe) (page 273). And the list goes on, with stews and *tielle*, dishes that happily combine rice with mussels (page 275), potatoes with cuttlefish or squid (page 276), and potatoes with horseradish. Worthy of mention are the sublime Burrata di Andria and the intriguing flavor of lampascioni, grape hyacinth bulbs. When it comes to desserts, the pleasant bitterness of almonds marries wonderfully with the warm, sweetness of Aleatico di Puglia, a deep garnet-colored dessert wine with violet tinges and a delicate perfume.

Taralli

A classic Puglian snack, these savory durum wheat crackers are boiled then baked for a unique texture, and served all day long, though most commonly as an appetizer alongside an aperitivo.

PREPARATION TIME 25 minutes
COOKING TIME 1 hour
RESTING TIME 3 hours
SERVES 6

2½ fl oz/⅓ cup/70 ml extra-virgin olive oil
1¾ fl oz/scant ¼ cup/50 ml white wine
9 ounces/generous 2 cups/250 g "0" flour
Heaping teaspoon of fine salt

Place the oil, wine and 1¾ fl oz/scant ¼ cup/50 ml water in a bowl and emulsify using a fork. Add the sifted flour and knead.

After a couple of minutes, add the salt and work well with your hands until you obtain a smooth and compact ball. Place it in a bowl covered with plastic wrap (cling film) and let it rest for an hour.

After resting, take the dough and divide it into 4-inch/10-cm strips with a diameter of approximately ½ inch/1.25 cm, which will give you the typical shape when you close them with the pressure of a finger (or,

as per the Apulian tradition, with a key—place one edge of dough on top of the other and apply pressure with the tubular part of the key, the end part not the handle, so as to create a small cut on the dough).

Meanwhile, bring a pan of water to a boil, and cook the taralli four or five at a time; as soon as they float to the surface, drain them and leave them to dry on a clean cloth, taking care to turn them over so they don't stick. Let them dry for a couple of hours and, once dry, place them on a baking tray and bake at 400 °F/200 °C/180 °C Fan/Gas 6 for 30 minutes until completely golden.

Orecchiette with cime di rapa

Puglia's most iconic pasta dish. The origins of orecchiette are unclear, though the Pugliese say that the shape echoes the *trulli,* the traditional conical huts of the region.

PREPARATION TIME 1 hour
COOKING TIME 15 minutes
DRYING TIME 1 hour
SERVES 6

7 ounces/1¼ cups/200g semolina flour
14 ounces/3¼ cups/400 g "00" flour, plus extra for dusting
Pinch of salt
Grated Parmesan, to serve

FOR THE SAUCE
2 pounds 4 ounces/1 kg cime di rapa (broccoli rabe)
3½ fl oz/scant ½ cup/100 ml olive oil
1 small red chile, seeded and sliced
2 cloves garlic, finely sliced
4–5 anchovy fillets
Salt and black pepper

Mix both types of flour in a large bowl, make a well in the center, then add a pinch of salt to the well. Add enough lukewarm water to form a dough when mixed, then knead until smooth and dense. Place the dough on a lightly floured work surface and cut it into eight equal pieces. Roll each piece into a cylinder about 1 inch/ 2.5 cm in diameter and cover with a cloth. Slice one cylinder at a time into circles, about ¼ inch/5 mm thick. Place the back of a knife on the edge of a circle and pull the dough toward you so that it curls around the blade. When you have rolled all the circles in this way, stretch each of them over the end of your thumb to make the shape of a little ear. Continue until the dough is used up. Set aside to dry for about 1 hour.

Cook the orecchiette in a large saucepan of boiling salted water for 2–3 minutes until al dente. Drain and set aside.

Cook the cime di rapa (broccoli rabe) in another large saucepan of boiling salted water for 1 minute, then drain well. Heat some of the oil in a skillet (frying pan), add the cime di rapa, and fry for 2–3 minutes until cooked through. Season well.

Heat the remaining oil in a separate skillet, add half the chile, and fry for 1–2 minutes until softened. Add the garlic and fry until fragrant. Stir in the anchovies, breaking them up, then add the cooked orecchiette and cime di rapa and stir well. Season to taste. Transfer to a serving dish and serve with grated Parmesan.

Pasta timbale

Definitely a dish to save for special occasions, but well worth the effort when you do make it. It is named for the mold in which it's cooked—the *timballo*—which has a diameter equal to its height.

PREPARATION TIME 1 hour

COOKING TIME 2 hours

STANDING TIME 1 hour 15 minutes

SERVES 8–10

3 eggplants (aubergines), peeled and sliced

Vegetable oil, for frying

2 eggs, beaten

3½ ounces/1½ cups/100 g dried bread crumbs

9 ounces/250 g penne pasta

4 tablespoons grated Parmesan cheese

5½ ounces/150 g mozzarella cheese, sliced

Salt

FOR THE MEAT SAUCE

14 ounces/400 g pork slices

2 tablespoons grated Parmesan cheese

3½ ounces/100 g cured ham slices

3½ fl oz/scant ½ cup/100 ml red wine

28 fl oz/3¼ cups/800 ml tomato sauce

Hot chicken stock (optional)

Black pepper

FOR THE MEATBALLS

5 oz/150 g ground (minced) veal

1 egg yolk

2oz/½ cup/50 g grated Parmesan cheese

Vegetable oil or stock

FOR THE PASTRY

1 pound 2 ounces/4 cups/500 g all-purpose (plain) flour,
   plus extra for dusting

7 ounces/scant 1 cup/200 g lard or butter

2 ounces/¼ cup/50 g sugar

5 egg yolks

4 tablespoons dry white wine

Place the eggplant (aubergine) slices in a colander, sprinkle with salt, and leave for about 1 hour to expel their excess moisture. Rinse, drain, and squeeze dry.

Heat a 1-inch/2.5-cm depth of the oil for frying in a sauté pan. Place the eggs and bread crumbs in separate shallow bowls. When the oil is hot, dip some eggplant slices into the egg, then in the bread crumbs until coated all over, and fry a few at a time until golden. Drain on paper towels.

To make the sauce, place the pork slices on a chopping board and beat with a rolling pin or heavy-bottomed saucepan until thin. Season them, then sprinkle them with the Parmesan. Cover with the ham slices, then roll up and secure with toothpicks (cocktail sticks).

Heat a little oil in a large skillet (frying pan), add the meat rolls, and brown on all sides. Drizzle the wine over them, allow it to evaporate, then add the tomato sauce and simmer for 10 minutes, adding a little hot stock if the mixture seems too thick. Set aside to cool, then remove the toothpicks and coarsely chop the meat rolls. Return to the skillet and cook over a high heat for 5 minutes to reduce the sauce until thickened.

Meanwhile, cook the pasta in a large saucepan of boiling salted water for 10 minutes, or until al dente. Drain and mix with the meat sauce and half the grated Parmesan.

To make the meatballs, put the ground veal in a bowl, add the egg yolk, cheese, and a little salt and pepper and mix well. Shape the mixture into walnut-sized meatballs. Fry in hot oil for 5–7 minutes until they are golden brown, or boil in stock for 5 minutes.

Preheat the oven to 350 °F/180 °C/160 °C Fan/ Gas 4. Grease a 10-inch/26-cm ring mold and place on a baking sheet.

To make the pastry, place the flour in a mound on a clean work counter, make a well in the center, and add the lard, sugar, egg yolks, and wine. Knead until you have a smooth dough. Cut off two-thirds, place on a lightly floured counter, and shape into a ball. Flatten slightly, then roll into a circle and use to line the prepared mold.

Arrange alternating layers of the pasta, eggplant, mozzarella, meatballs, and remaining Parmesan in the pastry case, finishing with a layer of eggplant. Roll out the remaining pastry and use to cover the filled mold, pressing the edges firmly together. Trim off the excess, then brush the surface with a little beaten egg.

Cut a small hole in the center of the pie and insert a "chimney"—for example, a cannoli tube—in order to release steam during cooking. Brush again with beaten egg and bake for about 1 hour, until golden brown. When done, leave to stand for 15 minutes, then remove the ring, slide the timbale onto a plate and serve.

Baked squid and potatoes

A quick and easy second course in which the squid and potatoes are baked together, infusing them with all the traditional flavors of Puglia. This dish can also be made with cuttlefish, if preferred.

PREPARATION TIME 20 minutes

COOKING TIME 30–40 minutes

SERVES 6–8

2 pounds 4 ounces/1 kg squid, cleaned
2 tablespoons olive oil
1 small onion, sliced
1 clove garlic, chopped
5 ripe tomatoes, skinned, seeded, and chopped
2 tablespoons chopped parsley
1 pound 2 ounces/500 g potatoes, peeled and cut into wedges
Salt and black pepper

FOR THE STUFFING
7 ounces/2 cups/200 g bread crumbs
2½ ounces/¾ cup/65 g grated Parmesan or pecorino cheese
1 egg
6 tablespoons chopped parsley

Preheat the oven to 400 °F/200 °C/180 °C Fan/Gas 6.

To make the stuffing, place the bread crumbs in a large bowl with the cheese, egg, parsley, and seasoning. Mix well, then spoon the stuffing into the cavities of the squid and secure each one with a toothpick (cocktail stick).

Pour the oil into a large baking dish, then arrange the onion, garlic, and half the tomatoes on top. Sprinkle with 1 tablespoon of the parsley and some salt. Sit the squid on top, arrange the potato wedges around the edge of the dish, then add the remaining tomatoes and parsley. Season and bake in the preheated oven for 30–40 minutes until the potatoes are tender. Leave to stand for a few minutes before serving.

Lamb with aromatic herbs

Agnello alle erbe aromatiche

Lamb is very popular in Puglia, perhaps because it was traditionally one of the cheaper meats. The rocky landscape of the region is ideal for sheep farming.

PREPARATION TIME 30 minutes
COOKING TIME 1 hour 25 minutes
MARINATING TIME 15 minutes
SERVES 6

3½ fl oz/scant ½ cup/100 ml red wine vinegar
2 tablespoons chopped rosemary
2 tablespoons chopped sage leaves
2 bay leaves
1 ounce/¼ cup/30 g all-purpose (plain) flour
3 pounds/1.5 kg shoulder of lamb, cut into 1½-inch/4-cm pieces
3–4 tablespoons olive oil
1 clove garlic, peeled and left whole
3 anchovy fillets, chopped
1 pound 2 ounces/500 g tomatoes, skinned, seeded, and diced
Salt and black pepper

Pour the vinegar into a medium bowl, add the chopped herbs and bay leaves, and leave to macerate for 15 minutes. Remove and discard the bay leaves.

Spread the flour out on a large plate, or put it in a plastic bag, add the lamb, season, and toss to coat. Shake to remove any excess flour.

Heat the oil in a large ovenproof saucepan with lid or Dutch oven (casserole), add the garlic clove, and fry until browned. Remove and discard the garlic, then add the anchovies and stir until they disintegrate. Add the lamb pieces and brown thoroughly on all sides. Pour the vinegar mixture over the meat and heat until the vinegar has evaporated. Season to taste.

Add the tomatoes to the lamb. Cover with a lid and cook for about 1 hour, or until the meat is tender. Alternatively, the casserole dish can be placed in an oven preheated to 300 °F/150 °C/130 °C Fan/Gas 2 and cooked for 1 hour. Taste and adjust the seasoning. Transfer to a warmed serving dish and serve.

Honey pastries

Cartellate are a Puglian holiday dessert—the preparation is a real labor of love, as you cut and twist the dough strips into rose shapes, and families gather to make these together in the lead-up to Christmas.

PREPARATION TIME 40 minutes
COOKING TIME 30 minutes
RISING TIME 4 hours
MAKES 8 large or 16 small pastries

1 pound 2 ounces/4 cups/500 g all-purpose (plain) flour, plus extra for dusting
¼ ounce/7 g quick rise (easy blend) yeast
3½ fl oz/scant ½ cup/100 ml olive oil
3½ fl oz/scant ½ cup/100 ml white wine
Vegetable oil, for deep-frying
12 ounces/1½ cups/350 g honey
Salt
Colored sprinkles, to decorate

Gather the flour in a mound on a work surface and make a well in the center. Add a pinch of salt, the yeast, oil, wine, and 4 fl oz/½ cup/120 ml lukewarm water to the well and quickly work into the flour until you have a soft, not sticky, dough. Knead for 5–10 minutes until the dough is smooth. Cover with plastic wrap (cling film) and leave to rise in a warm place for 2 hours, or until doubled in size.

Divide the dough into eight equal pieces, place them on a lightly floured work surface, and roll into balls. Using a rolling pin, roll them into very thin circles with a diameter of 10–12 inches/25–30 cm. Using a pastry wheel, cut each circle into a long spiral strip, about 2 inches/5 cm wide.

Fold each strip in half lengthwise and roll into a loose spiral. The finished spiral should look roughly like a rose. Set aside for 2 hours at room temperature.

Heat enough oil for deep-frying in a large, deep saucepan to 350 °F/180 °C on a thermometer, or until a cube of bread browns in 30 seconds. Carefully drop the pastries into the hot oil, one at a time, and deep-fry for about 2 minutes, or until golden brown, turning over halfway through cooking. Scoop out with a slotted spoon and drain on paper towels.

Heat the honey in a small saucepan. Using tongs, quickly dip the pastries into the warm honey, then arrange them on a platter and drizzle over more honey, if desired. Decorate with colored sprinkles and serve warm.

Calabria

The pleasure of concentrated flavors

Here we sample the flavors of Calabria, a name that in the Greek of Byzantium means "land of every good," which therefore applies to Cirò, the magnificent wine once given as a prize to the winning athletes at the Olympic Games. Calabria is located at the very tip of the boot of Italy, a land of coasts and mountains that is 155 miles (250 kilometers) long and bounded by the Ionian and Tyrrhenian seas. As a result, the cuisine of the region alternates between rustic and hearty dishes, such as pasta with concentrated lamb and pork sauces (page 284) and pita flatbreads stuffed with savory fillings; richly flavored seafood, such as the swordfish caught between Scilla and Bagnara; and vegetables in large mixed salads, casseroles of tomatoes and peppers, and pumpkin and zucchini (courgettes). And, under Calabria's bright sun, it reveals flavors of great contrasts, such as the fiery heat of the ubiquitous chile pepper and the soft sweetness of raw Tropea onions, which can also be wonderfully caramelized and enjoyed with fresh ricotta cheese, or the firm texture and spicy flavor of caciocavallo cheese set against the tender sweetness of Sibari figs. These are the unique flavors of Italian cuisine that are impossible to replicate.

'Nduja fileja

A flavorful dish of rich tomato sauce and spicy sausage. Fileja—meaning "little threads"—is a traditional pasta typical of the Vibo Valentia area, although it has become popular throughout Calabria.

PREPARATION TIME 10 minutes

COOKING TIME 30 minutes

SERVES 4

Extra-virgin olive oil, for cooking
3½ ounces/100 g 'nduja sausage
1 clove garlic, peeled and left whole
14 ounces/400 g tomatoes, skinned
10 ounces/280 g fresh or dried fileja
3 tablespoons grated aged pecorino cheese, preferably from
    Monte Poro, plus extra to serve (optional)
A few basil leaves
Salt

Heat a little oil in a large saucepan with a lid together with the 'nduja and garlic clove over a medium heat, and stir until the 'nduja melts. This will take a few minutes. Add the tomatoes and crush them with a wooden spoon to a coarse sauce. Stir well, reduce the heat to low, cover with a lid, and cook for at least 15–20 minutes, stirring occasionally.

Meanwhile, cook the pasta in another large pan of boiling salted water until it is slightly al dente to preserve its rustic texture. Drain the pasta, add to the sauce, and mix well.

Add the grated cheese, then add a few basil leaves and cook for a few more minutes over a very low heat. Divide between serving plates and serve immediately with more grated cheese, if desired.

Maltagliati with onions

Maltagliata con salsa di cipolel

The Tropea onion is mainly cultivated in the province of Vibo Valentia. Its sweet taste is due to the consistent year-round mild temperatures, the silty soil, and the proximity of the sea.

PREPARATION TIME 50 minutes

COOKING TIME 40 minutes

RESTING TIME 15 minutes

SERVES 4

7 ounces/1⅔ cups/200 g Italian "00" flour
2 eggs
Salt and black pepper

FOR THE SAUCE
1 pound 2 ounces/500 g red onions, preferably Tropea onions,
   thinly sliced
2–3 tablespoons olive oil
5–6 basil leaves

To make the pasta, gather the flour in a mound on a work surface and make a well in the center. Add the eggs to the well and sprinkle with a pinch of salt. Mix, then knead the dough for 10 minutes. Gather it into a ball, wrap the dough in plastic wrap (cling film), and leave to rest at room temperature for 15 minutes. Using a rolling pin, roll out the dough into a relatively thin sheet, then cut it into irregular diamond shapes with a knife.

For the sauce, pour 3½ fl oz/scant ½ cup/100 ml water into a large saucepan, add the thinly sliced onions, and cook over a low heat for 30 minutes. Mash the onions with the tines of a fork to a creamy consistency. When all the water has evaporated, add the oil and basil leaves, and season with a pinch of pepper.

Cook the pasta in a large saucepan of boiling salted water until al dente. Drain, transfer to the sauce, and mix so that it absorbs the flavor. Transfer the pasta to a serving dish and season with a sprinkling of pepper.

Linguine with sea urchins

Linguine ai ricci di mare

Spiny sea urchins are a Calabrian delicacy, cooked very quickly to preserve their taste and texture. Their preparation may be quite intricate, but this pasta dish with the scent of the sea is worth it.

PREPARATION TIME 30 minutes

COOKING TIME 25 minutes

SERVES 6

1¾ fl oz/scant ¼ cup/50 ml olive oil

1 clove garlic, peeled and left whole

1 pound 2 ounces/500 g ripe but firm tomatoes, skinned, seeded, and chopped

30 sea urchins

1 pound 2 ounces/500 g linguine

Salt and black pepper

Heat the oil in a large skillet (frying pan), add the garlic, and sauté until it turns golden, then remove and discard it. Add the tomatoes and season with salt and pepper. Add a ladleful of water and cook for 15 minutes.

Meanwhile, to prepare the sea urchins, carefully open them by splitting them in half, scoop out the tongues of roe with a teaspoon, and set them aside in a bowl.

Cook the pasta in a large saucepan of boiling salted water for 10 minutes, or until al dente. Drain, setting aside some of the cooking water. Add the pasta to the sauce in the pan along with the sea urchin roe and toss for a few seconds, adding a splash of the pasta cooking water, if necessary. Transfer the pasta to a serving dish and serve immediately.

Bell peppers with bread crumbs

A quick and colorful recipe to liven up the summer dining table. Red, yellow, and green bell peppers are cooked with bread crumbs, pecorino cheese, and capers in this tasty Calabrian dish.

PREPARATION TIME 20 minutes

COOKING TIME 40 minutes

SERVES 4–6

8 red, yellow, and green bell peppers

3 tablespoons extra-virgin olive oil

3 tablespoons dried bread crumbs

3 ounces/⅔ cup/80 g grated pecorino cheese

2 tablespoons capers in oil, drained

Pinch of dried oregano, plus extra to serve

Salt

Cut the bell peppers in half lengthwise, remove the ribs and seeds, then cut them into individual lobes. Heat the oil in a large pan, add the bell peppers, and cook for 20–25 minutes, or until they have softened slightly.

Sprinkle the bell peppers with the bread crumbs, followed by the cheese, capers, and oregano, and cook for another 15 minutes, turning them occasionally and moistening with a little hot water, if necessary. When cooked, adjust the seasoning with salt, sprinkle with more oregano as desired, and serve.

Saffron vegetable stew

Ciambotta allo zafferano

A southern Italian take on the ubiquitous Mediterranean dish of stewed vegetables, the recipe for which varies slightly from region to region. Saffron is one of Calabria's oldest crops, and is the star here.

PREPARATION TIME 45 minutes

COOKING TIME 1 hour

SERVES 8

1 sachet saffron threads
3 bell peppers
3 potatoes, peeled and cut into slices, about ⅛ in/3–4 mm thick
5½ fl oz/generous ⅔ cup/160 ml olive oil
3 eggplants (aubergines), diced
4 zucchini (courgettes), diced
1 onion, thinly sliced
2 cloves garlic, peeled and left whole
1 sprig rosemary
Pinch of dried oregano
1 pound 5 ounces/600 g tomatoes, skinned, seeded, and diced
1 tablespoon chopped parsley
1 tablespoon chopped basil
Salt

Add the saffron threads to a cup and pour over a little warm water. Set aside.

Using tongs, hold the bell peppers over a gas burner for 10 minutes, turning them frequently until the skins are blackened and blistered all over. Set aside to cool, then peel, remove the ribs and seeds, and cut them into strips. Set aside.

Cook the potatoes in a large saucepan of lightly salted water for 2–3 minutes, then drain and set aside.

Heat 3½ fl oz/scant ½ cup/100 ml of the oil in a large skillet (frying pan), add the peppers, and fry for 6–7 minutes. Remove to a plate, then add the diced eggplants (aubergines) and zucchini (courgettes) and fry for 10 minutes. Remove and set aside.

Heat the remaining oil in another skillet, add the onion and garlic, and fry until lightly colored. Add the rosemary, oregano, and saffron and stir. After a few minutes, add the tomatoes and cook for 10 minutes. Add the eggplants (aubergines) and zucchini (courgettes), then after a few minutes, add the potatoes. Taste and adjust the seasoning with salt, add a ladleful of water, and cook until the potatoes are cooked through.

Remove the pan from the heat, take out and discard the rosemary and garlic, and transfer the vegetables to a serving dish. Sprinkle with parsley and basil before serving.

Pan-fried anchovies with oregano

A coming together of three traditional Calabrian ingredients—the freshest anchovies, wild dried oregano, and warm, spicy red chiles—to create a simple yet unforgettable dish.

PREPARATION TIME 40 minutes

COOKING TIME 30 minutes

SERVES 6

All-purpose (plain) flour, for coating

2 pounds 4 ounces/1 kg fresh anchovies, gutted and boned

Olive oil, for frying

2 cloves garlic, chopped

1 red chile, chopped

2 tablespoons chopped fresh oregano

1 tablespoon chopped parsley

1 dried bay leaf

3½ fl oz/scant ½ cup/100 ml white wine vinegar

7 ounces/200 g cherry tomatoes, chopped

Salt

Spread the flour out on a large plate, add the anchovies, and toss in the flour until coated. Heat some oil in a large skillet (frying pan), add the fish, and fry for 2–3 minutes on both sides until golden brown. Remove them from the pan and drain on paper towels.

Heat 2 tablespoons of oil in a large pan and cover the bottom with a layer of fried anchovies. Sprinkle with the garlic, chile, oregano, and parsley, then add the bay leaf and cook for a few minutes, shaking the pan frequently.

Drizzle the anchovies with the vinegar and let it evaporate, then add the chopped tomatoes and season with a pinch of salt. Cook for 10 minutes, or until the tomatoes are cooked through. Remove from the heat and serve the anchovies hot or cold.

Marinated leg of lamb

A rustic second-course dish of marinated pancetta-studded lamb cooked low and slow, then served on a bed of olives and cipollini onions with a rich sauce alongside.

PREPARATION TIME 20 minutes
COOKING TIME 2 hours
MARINATING TIME 4 hours
SERVES 8

1 large leg of lamb
7 ounces/200 g pancetta, half cut into matchsticks and half cut into cubes
3 cloves garlic, crushed
1 small sprig rosemary
2 bay leaves
1 dried chile, crumbled
1 teaspoon black peppercorns
7 fl oz/scant 1 cup/200 ml dry white wine
All-purpose (plain) flour, for coating
5 fl oz/scant ⅔ cup/150 ml olive oil
10½ ounces/3¾ cups/300 g pitted green olives
1 pound 9 ounces/700 g cipollini onions
Meat broth (stock), to cover
Salt

Make small incisions all over the lamb leg and insert the pancetta matchsticks into it. Place the lamb leg in a large bowl and add the crushed garlic, herbs, crumbled chile, and peppercorns, then cover the meat with the wine. Cover the bowl with plastic wrap (cling film) and leave to marinate in the refrigerator for at least 4 hours.

Preheat the oven to 350 °F/180 °C/160 °C Fan/Gas 4.

Drain and dry the lamb leg with paper towels. Spread the flour out on a large plate and toss the lamb in it until coated. Heat the oil in a large ovenproof pan, add the lamb, and cook until browned all over. Add the cubed pancetta, olives, and onions, and sauté until well colored. Add enough broth (stock) to just cover the contents of the pan and bring to a boil, then transfer the pan to the oven and cook in the preheated oven for 1½ hours, or until the meat is fully cooked.

Remove the pan from the oven and transfer the lamb leg, olives, and onions to a serving dish and keep warm. Set the pan with the remaining broth on the heat and reduce it for a few minutes, then pour the hot sauce over the leg and serve.

St. Joseph's choux pastries

Delicious donut-shaped fried choux pastries topped with pastry cream and Amarena cherries, made to celebrate the feast of Saint Joseph on March 19, which is also Father's Day in Italy.

PREPARATION TIME 40 minutes

COOKING TIME 45 minutes

MAKES 6–7

½ batch pastry cream (page 252)
3½ ounces/generous ¾ cup/100 g Italian "00" flour
2 ounces/50 g unsalted butter
½ ounce/15 g superfine (caster) sugar
Pinch of salt
2½ ounces/75 g eggs, beaten
2½ ounces/75 g egg whites
Vegetable oil, for deep-frying
Confectioners' (icing) sugar, for dusting
6–7 Amarena cherries in syrup, drained

Make the pastry cream, cover it with plastic wrap (cling film), and set aside to cool.

To make the choux pastry, sift the flour into a bowl. Pour 4 fl oz/½ cup/125 ml water into a large saucepan, add the butter, superfine (caster) sugar, and salt, and bring to a boil. Remove from the heat and add all the sifted flour at once while stirring with a whisk.

Return the pan to the heat and cook, stirring continuously, until the resulting paste has dried out. It is ready when it comes away from the sides of the pan, begins to sizzle, and a light white veil appears on the bottom of the pan. Remove from the heat and set aside to cool.

Transfer the cooled paste to a stand mixer fitted with a dough hook and, while beating, add the beaten eggs and egg whites, a little at a time, until they are all incorporated.

Preheat the oven to 400 °F/200 °C/180 °C Fan/Gas 6. Line a large baking sheet with parchment paper.

When the choux pastry is shiny, smooth, and sticky, with a ribbon-like texture, transfer it to a pastry (piping) bag fitted with a ⅝-inch (15-mm) star tip. Pipe the zeppole, each comprising two overlapping rings, onto the prepared baking sheet, then bake in the preheated oven for 25–30 minutes until they detach themselves from the parchment paper.

Heat enough oil for deep-frying in a large, deep saucepan to 340 °F/170 °C on a thermometer, or until a cube of bread browns in 30 seconds. As soon as the pastries are cooked, carefully add them to the hot oil and deep-fry, turning them over, until golden brown on all sides. Using a slotted spoon, remove them from the pan and drain on paper towels.

Top the fried pastries with a generous dollop of pastry cream, dust with confectioners' (icing) sugar, and crown the center of each pastry with an Amarena cherry.

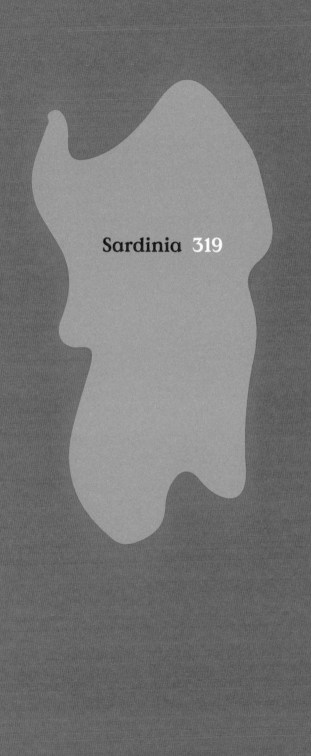

Sardinia 319

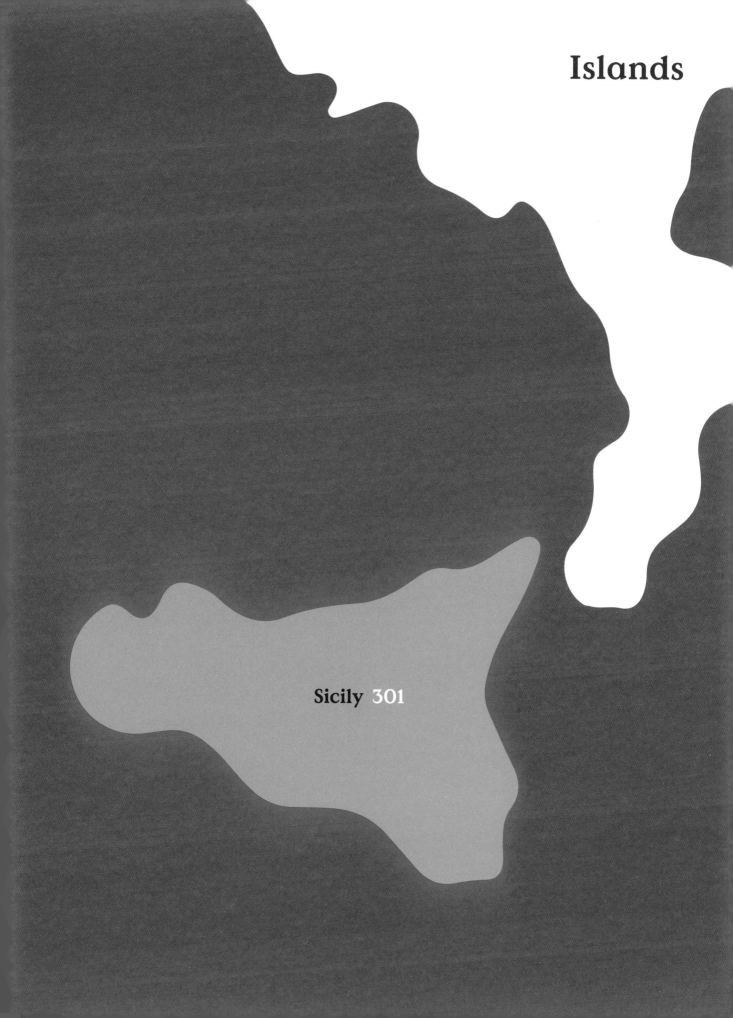

Sicily 301

Sicily

A festival of sunny cuisine

The taste of Sicily moves with wonderful ease from one excess to another—from savory to sweet to sour—or combines everything into a celebration of flavors that are a symphony of the sun. It is where intriguing citrus salads featuring slices of juicy oranges or equally juicy lemons are dressed with a drizzle of oil, a sprinkling of black pepper, and a pinch of salt (page 308). And where pasta is combined with sardines (page 305): the versions from Palermo and Catania, albeit with slight differences, both boast the flavors of the island that are first "cooked" by the sun and air, light and wind, turning tomatoes into little mouthfuls of nectar, while eggplants (aubergines), known as *le belle* ("beautiful ones") form the soft notes of caponata (page 311), an absolute triumph of pan-fried vegetables that demands the sharpness of capers. Fish is found in abundance, from the smallest ones of little value that are washed ashore after storms, known as *fragagghia*, which are recovered to be deep-fried, to the highly prized, such as swordfish and tuna of the highest quality. Other emotions are aroused by tasting the region's desserts. The pastry tradition of Sicily is truly the most extraordinary, mouthwatering, and ancient of Italy, which includes cannoli filled with creamy ricotta (page 314). And let us not overlook the traditional granitas (page 317) and sorbets. Finally, green Smeraldo di Bronte pistachios lend themselves to the most intriguing sweet and savory culinary combinations.

Arancini

One of the most famous Italian street foods, this Sicilian specialty is an irresistible treat at any time of the day, though they are exceptional when eaten hot, freshly fried, with a crunchy outside and soft filling.

PREPARATION TIME 2 hours
COOKING TIME 30–40 minutes
SERVES 6

11 ounces/1¾ cups/300 g risotto rice, such as Arborio
3½ ounces/generous ¾ cup/100 g grated sharp (mature) caciocavallo cheese
5 ounces/150 g mozzarella cheese, cut into cubes
2 eggs
3 ounces/1⅔ cups/80 g bread crumbs
Olive or vegetable oil, for deep-frying
Salt

FOR THE MEAT SAUCE
7 ounces/1 cup/200 g shelled peas
1½ ounces/3 tablespoons/40 g butter
2 tablespoons olive oil
½ onion, chopped
9 ounces/2 cups/250 g ground (minced) beef
2 tablespoons dry white wine
1 tablespoon tomato paste (purée)
Salt and black pepper

Cook the rice in a large saucepan of boiling salted water for 15–20 minutes until al dente, then drain. Transfer to a bowl, stir in the grated cheese, and set aside to cool.

Meanwhile, for the meat sauce, cook the peas in a saucepan of boiling water for 5 minutes, then drain and set aside. Melt the butter with the oil in another pan, add the onion, and cook over a low heat, stirring occasionally, for 5 minutes, or until softened. Add the minced (ground) beef, increase the heat to medium, and cook, stirring frequently, until lightly browned. Add the wine and cook until the alcohol has evaporated, then mix the tomato paste (purée) with a little water in a small bowl and stir into the pan. Season to taste with salt and pepper, cover with a lid, and simmer over a low heat for 20 minutes. Add the peas, cover again, and simmer for another 10 minutes.

For the croquettes, take a little rice and put it into the palm of your left hand, then shape it to resemble a small, slightly pointed orange with your right hand. Make a small hollow in the center with your right thumb and fill with a teaspoon of meat sauce and a cube of mozzarella, then cover with the rice.

Beat the eggs with a pinch of salt in a shallow dish and spread out the bread crumbs in another dish. Heat enough oil for deep-frying in a large, deep saucepan to 350 °F/180 °C on a thermometer, or until a cube of bread browns in 30 seconds. Dip the croquettes first into the beaten egg, then in the bread crumbs to coat. Add them to the hot oil, in batches, and cook until lightly golden brown. Using a slotted spoon, remove them from the pan and drain on paper towels, then transfer to a warmed serving dish. Keep hot while you cook the remaining batches. Serve hot.

Pasta with sardines

A dish made with the bounty of ingredients found across Sicily—both on land and from the sea. This is a classic dish of the region, in which the "sauce" is quite rustic and contains no cheese.

PREPARATION TIME 1 hour 10 minutes
COOKING TIME 1 hour 15 minutes
SOAKING TIME 15 minutes
SERVES 6–8

3 ounces/½ cup/80 g golden raisins (sultanas)
4 oil-packed anchovy fillets
Milk, for soaking the anchovies
6 bunches wild fennel
1 pound 2 ounces/500 g fresh sardines, scaled, cleaned, and boned
All-purpose (plain) flour, for dusting
5 fl oz/scant ⅔ cup/150 ml olive oil, plus extra for drizzling

1 clove garlic, finely chopped
1 tablespoon chopped parsley, plus extra to garnish
Pinch of saffron threads, lightly crushed
1 onion, coarsely chopped
3 ounces/¾ cup/80 g pine nuts
1 pound 2 ounces/500 g maccheroncini
Salt and black pepper

Place the golden raisins (sultanas) in a small bowl, cover with warm water, and leave to soak for 10 minutes, then drain and squeeze out. Set aside. Place the anchovies in another bowl, cover in milk, and leave to soak for 5 minutes, then drain and chop into pieces. Set aside.

Bring a large saucepan of salted water to a boil, add the wild fennel, bring back to a boil, and simmer for 15 minutes. Remove with a slotted spoon and pat dry with paper towels, then chop finely. Set aside the cooking water.

Dust half the sardines with flour, shaking off the excess. Heat half the oil in a large skillet (frying pan), add the floured sardines, and cook, turning once, until evenly browned, then remove from the heat.

Heat 2 tablespoons of the oil with the garlic and parsley in a shallow pan, add the remaining sardines, pour in 100 ml/3½ fl oz (scant ½ cup) water, and simmer for 10–15 minutes. Mix the saffron with a little water in a small bowl, then add to the pan, season with salt and pepper,

and stir to break up the sardines. Simmer for 10 minutes, then remove from the heat and set aside.

Put the onion, remaining oil, and 100 ml/3½ fl oz (scant ½ cup) water in another shallow pan and cook for 5 minutes. Add the wild fennel, golden raisins, pine nuts, and anchovies and simmer for 10 minutes.

Meanwhile, bring the reserved cooking water to a boil in a large saucepan, add the pasta, bring back to a boil, and cook for 8–10 minutes until al dente. Drain, return to the pan, and drizzle with olive oil. Stir in the saffron sauce and onion and fennel mixture.

Preheat the oven to 180 °C/350 °F/Gas Mark 4.

Make alternate layers of pasta and fried sardines in a large ovenproof dish, ending with a layer of pasta. Bake in the preheated oven for 15 minutes, then remove, sprinkle with parsley, and serve.

Pasta alla Norma

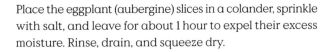

A rich eggplant (aubergine) and tomato-based pasta dish, which originated in Catania, and is said to have been named by Sicilian playwright Nino Martoglio for Bellini's opera of the same name.

PREPARATION TIME 30 minutes
COOKING TIME 45 minutes
RESTING TIME 1 hour
SERVES 4

2 small eggplants (aubergines), sliced
2 tablespoons olive oil, plus extra for deep-frying
1 clove garlic, peeled and left whole
12 ounces/350 g fresh tomatoes, chopped, or 1 pound
  2 ounces/500 g puréed strained tomatoes (passata)
12 ounces/350 g penne pasta
3½ ounces/generous ¾ cup/100 g grated hard ricotta cheese
8 basil leaves
Salt and black pepper

Place the eggplant (aubergine) slices in a colander, sprinkle with salt, and leave for about 1 hour to expel their excess moisture. Rinse, drain, and squeeze dry.

Heat the oil for deep-frying in a large, deep saucepan to 350 °F/180 °C on a thermometer, or until a cube of bread browns in 30 seconds. Add the eggplants in batches and deep-fry for 8–10 minutes until golden brown. Remove with a slotted spoon and drain on paper towels. Keep warm.

Heat the 2 tablespoons of oil in a shallow pan, add the garlic, and sauté for a few minutes until lightly browned, then remove and discard it. Add the fresh tomatoes, if using, and cook, shaking the pan occasionally, for 10 minutes, until softened and pulpy, then season to taste with salt and pepper. Alternatively, add the puréed strained tomatoes (passata), season to taste with salt and pepper, and cook until heated through.

Meanwhile, cook the pasta in a large saucepan of boiling salted water for 10 minutes, or until al dente. Drain and tip into a large serving dish. Sprinkle with half the grated ricotta, spoon half the tomato sauce on top, and add the basil leaves. Top with the eggplant slices, sprinkle with the remaining ricotta, and cover with the remaining tomato sauce. Serve immediately.

Trapani-style couscous

Couscous was introduced to Sicily by its Arabian ancestors, and also simply due to the island's close proximity to Africa. The dish is traditionally steamed in a terracotta pot called a couscoussier.

PREPARATION TIME 1 hour
COOKING TIME 1 hour 30 minutes
SERVES 6–8

FOR THE FISH BROTH
6 black peppercorns
1 onion, peeled and left whole
2 bay leaves
2 sprigs parsley
Pinch of saffron threads
4 pounds 8 ounces/2 kg mixed fish (scorpion fish, grouper, sea bream, conger eel), cleaned
Salt

FOR THE COUSCOUS
2 pounds 4 ounces/5¾ cups/1 kg couscous

FOR THE SAUCE
1 onion, very thinly sliced
1 clove garlic, peeled and left whole
2 tablespoons olive oil
1 pound 12 ounces/800 g tomatoes, coarsely chopped
2 ounces/generous ⅓ cup/50 g blanched almonds
2 tablespoons chopped flat-leaf parsley
17 fl oz/2 cups/500 ml fish stock
Black pepper

FOR THE GARNISH
Olive oil, for frying
16 uncooked shrimp (prawns), shells intact
6–8 baby squid, cleaned and dusted in all-purpose (plain) flour

For the fish broth, pour 50 fl oz/6 cups/1.5 liters water into a large saucepan with a lid, add the peppercorns, onion, bay leaves, parsley, saffron, and salt, cover with a lid, and cook for 15 minutes. Add the fish to the pan and simmer for 30 minutes, then remove from the heat. Using a slotted spoon or skimmer, lift the fish out of the broth and remove and discard the skin and any bones. Flake the flesh and set aside. Strain the broth through a fine-mesh strainer (sieve) into a bowl.

Cook the couscous according to the packet directions, using the hot strained fish broth in place of water.

Meanwhile, for the sauce, pour water into a large skillet (frying pan) to a depth of 2½ inches/4 cm, add a pinch of salt, and heat to a simmer. Add the onion and garlic and cook until the liquid has evaporated, then add the olive oil and cook, stirring occasionally, for 5–8 minutes until the onion is lightly browned. Add the tomatoes, almonds, and parsley, season with salt and black pepper, and cook, occasionally mashing the tomatoes with a fork, for 15 minutes. Remove the pan from the heat and take out and discard the garlic.

Stir the fish, fish stock, and any leftover broth into the sauce, and cook over a medium heat until reduced and thickened.

Meanwhile, to prepare the garnish, heat plenty of oil in a pan, add the shrimp (prawns) and squid and cook for 5–8 minutes, until cooked through. Remove with a slotted spoon and drain on paper towels.

Place the couscous in a large serving dish and top with the fish, shrimp, and squid. Strain the sauce and serve alongside the couscous, for pouring.

Orange and fennel salad

The refreshing flavor of the juicy oranges and the crunch of the herbal fennel combine beautifully with the tasty piquancy of roast olives in this Sicilian citrus salad—a perfect accompaniment to meat dishes.

PREPARATION TIME 30 minutes

COOKING TIME 15 minutes

SERVES 8

3½ ounces/1 cup/100 g pitted black olives
Olive oil, for drizzling
8 oranges
3–4 fennel bulbs, thinly sliced, fronds set aside

FOR THE DRESSING
5 tablespoons olive oil
Juice of ½ lemon, strained
2 tablespoons chopped parsley
1 teaspoon fennel seeds (optional)
Salt and black pepper

Preheat the oven to 400 °F/200 °C/180 °C Fan/Gas 6.

Spread the olives out on a large baking sheet, drizzle with olive oil, and roast in the preheated oven for 15 minutes, or until heated through. Remove from the oven and set aside to cool.

For the dressing, add the olive oil, lemon juice, parsley, fennel fronds, and fennel seeds, if using, to a bowl and whisk together to emulsify. Season to taste with salt and pepper. Set aside.

Cut off the peel from the oranges, removing all traces of bitter white pith. Cut the flesh into circles, put them into a large salad bowl, and add the fennel and olives.

Drizzle the dressing over the salad, mix well, and serve immediately.

Caponata

Caponata classica

Another variation on a ratatouille-style dish, the difference in this Sicilian classic is the use of green olives and capers. Caponata is found on every menu across the island, with each town having its own version.

PREPARATION TIME 1 hour
COOKING TIME 1 hour 40 minutes
SERVES 4–6

3 tablespoons raisins
5 ounces/1¼ cups/150 g pitted green olives
3 ounces/90 g capers preserved in salt
3½ fl oz/scant ½ cup/100 ml white wine vinegar, plus extra for the capers
2 celery stalks
5 fl oz/scant ⅔ cup/150 ml olive oil
4 large round eggplants (aubergines), cut into cubes
1 onion, thinly sliced into rings

2–3 ounces/¼–scant ½ cup/50–80 g superfine (caster) sugar, plus extra as needed
14 ounces/1 cup/400 g puréed strained tomatoes (passata)
1 ounce/¼ cup/25 g pine nuts
1 sprig basil, thinly sliced
2 ounces/1 cup/50 g fresh bread crumbs
3 tablespoons blanched almonds, toasted and chopped
Salt

Place the raisins in a small bowl, cover with warm water, and leave to soak for 10 minutes, then drain and squeeze out. Cook the olives in a small saucepan of boiling water for 2 minutes, then drain and chop. Set aside. Rinse the capers in water acidulated with a little vinegar to remove the salt. Set aside.

Cook the celery stalks in a large saucepan of boiling water for a few minutes, then drain and cut into small pieces. Set aside.

Heat 5 tablespoons of the oil in a skillet (frying pan), add the eggplants (aubergines), and cook, stirring frequently, for 10 minutes, or until golden brown. Remove with a slotted spoon and drain on paper towels.

Heat 2 tablespoons of the remaining oil in a heavy-bottomed pan. Add the onion and cook over a low heat, stirring occasionally, for 10 minutes, or until golden. Stir in 3 tablespoons of the sugar and cook for another

10–20 minutes until caramelized. Remove the pan from the heat.

Heat the puréed strained tomatoes (passata) in a small pan, then stir in the vinegar and remaining sugar. Heat 2 tablespoons of the remaining oil in a large skillet, add the celery and caramelized onion, and cook over a low heat, stirring occasionally, for 5 minutes. Add the capers, olives, raisins, and pine nuts and cook, stirring occasionally, for a few minutes, then stir in the tomato sauce mixture, basil, and eggplants. Simmer for 15 minutes, then season to taste with salt and add more sugar if necessary. Remove the pan from the heat and transfer the caponata to a serving dish.

Heat the remaining oil in a small pan, add the bread crumbs, and cook over a medium heat, stirring frequently, for a few minutes until golden brown. Remove from the heat and sprinkle them over the caponata. Add the almonds and set aside to cool before serving.

Tuna with potatoes and honey sauce

Tonno con patate e salsa al miele

The island is known for its tuna fishing, both past and present, and here the fish is marinated, fried, and roasted before being served alongside golden fried potatoes and in an *agrodolce* ("sweet and sour") sauce.

PREPARATION TIME 30 minutes
COOKING TIME 50 minutes
MARINATING TIME 10 minutes
RESTING TIME 10 minutes
SERVES 6

6 × 200-g / 7-oz tuna slices
3–4 myrtle leaves, thinly sliced
1 clove garlic, thinly sliced
3 tablespoons olive oil, plus extra for drizzling
24 new potatoes
Salt and black pepper

FOR THE SAUCE
4 tomatoes, skinned and diced
1 tablespoon finely chopped flat-leaf parsley
1 tablespoon finely chopped chives
7 fl oz/scant 1 cup/200 ml red wine vinegar
4–5 tablespoons millefiori honey
2 tablespoons pine nuts, toasted

Preheat the oven to 400 °F/200 °C/180 °C Fan/Gas 6.

Place the tuna in a large bowl, season with salt and pepper, sprinkle with the myrtle leaves and garlic slices, drizzle lightly with oil, and leave to marinate in the refrigerator for 10 minutes.

Meanwhile, for the sauce, add the tomatoes to a large bowl and sprinkle with a little salt, a pinch of pepper, the parsley, and chives. Pour the vinegar into a medium saucepan, bring to a boil, and cook until it is reduced by a quarter. Stir in the honey, then remove from the heat and set aside to cool. When the vinegar mixture is cold, stir it into the tomatoes, add the pine nuts, and drizzle with oil. Taste and adjust the seasoning and leave to stand until ready to serve.

Heat the 3 tablespoons oil in a large skillet (frying pan), add the tuna slices, and cook for about 2 minutes on each side. Transfer the tuna to a roasting pan and roast in the preheated oven for 10 minutes, then remove from the oven and leave to stand for 10 minutes.

Cook the potatoes in a large saucepan of lightly salted boiling water for 10 minutes, then drain. Drizzle oil into a small skillet and heat over a medium heat. Add the potatoes and cook, turning occasionally, until golden and cooked through. Remove from the heat.

Arrange the slices of tuna in the center of a serving dish and spoon the potatoes around them. Pour the sauce over the fish and potatoes and serve.

Veal escalope with Marsala

Marsala is a town in the very west of Sicily, known throughout the world for its fortified wine, made using the local grapes. It is often used in cooking, as here, to create a rich, aromatic sauce.

PREPARATION TIME 10 minutes
COOKING TIME 30 minutes
SERVES 4

All-purpose (plain) flour, for dusting
1 pound 2 ounces/500 g/1 lb 2 oz veal scallops (escalopes)
3 ounces/¾ stick/80 g butter
14 fl oz/1¾ cups/400 ml dry Marsala
Salt
2 tablespoons chopped parsley, to garnish

Spread the flour out on a large plate and toss the veal in it until it is dusted with flour all over. Shake off the excess flour.

Melt the butter in a large skillet (frying pan) and heat over a high heat until it turns hazel in color. Add the veal, in batches if necessary, and cook for 5 minutes on each side until browned. Season to taste with salt, then reduce the heat to low and cook for a few more minutes. Remove the veal from the pan and set aside on a plate in a warm place.

Scrape up all the sediment from the bottom of the pan with a wooden spoon, then pour in the Marsala, stir well, and cook until reduced. Spoon the sauce over the veal, garnish with the parsley, and serve.

Cannoli

The traditional Sicilian cannolo consists of a crunchy shell with ricotta filling, dipped into pistachio nuts. The recipe calls for twenty or so metal cannoli tubes with which to mold the dough.

PREPARATION TIME 30 minutes
COOKING TIME 30 minutes
CHILLING TIME 12 hours
RESTING TIME 30 minutes
MAKES 20–22

5 ounces/1¼ cups/150 g all-purpose (plain) flour, plus extra
  for dusting
1 tablespoon lard
2 teaspoons white wine vinegar
3–4 tablespoons Malvasia wine
1 egg white, plus extra for brushing
1 teaspoon superfine (caster) sugar
Vegetable oil, for frying
Salt

FOR THE FILLING
2 pounds 4 ounces/4½ cups/1 kg Ricotta Romana (PDO) cheese
14 ounces/3¼ cups/400 g confectioners' (icing) sugar
2 ounces/50 g candied pumpkin, diced
3 ounces/80 g 70 % dark chocolate, finely chopped
2–3 tablespoons white rum

TO DECORATE
4–5 shelled pistachios, slivered
Vanilla-flavored confectioners' (icing) sugar, for dusting

For the filling, press the ricotta through a fine-mesh strainer (sieve) into a bowl, then add the confectioners' (icing) sugar and beat with a wooden spoon. Add the candied pumpkin, chocolate, and rum and mix well. Cover with plastic wrap (cling film) and leave to chill in the refrigerator for 12 hours.

To make the dough, sift the flour with a pinch of salt into a large bowl. Add the lard, vinegar, wine, egg white, and sugar and mix well to form a firm dough. Shape the dough into a ball, wrap in plastic wrap, and leave to rest for 30 minutes.

Cut the dough into 2–3 pieces and roll each out on a lightly floured work surface. Cut out 20–22 squares or stamp out rounds with a fluted pastry cutter. Put a cannoli

tube diagonally across each square, wrap the dough around it, and seal by brushing with a very small amount of beaten egg white.

Fill a skillet (frying pan) three-quarters of the way with vegetable oil and heat. Add the cannoli, seam side down, a few rolls at a time, and cook, turning once, for a few minutes, or until golden brown. Remove with a slotted spoon and drain on paper towels, then leave to stand until cool enough to handle. Remove the metal tubes and use a piping bag to fill the cannoli with the ricotta filling just before serving.

Spread the pistachio slivers out on a plate. Dust the cannoli with the vanilla confectioners' sugar, then dip both ends into the pistachios to decorate.

Coffee granita

Granita is a typical cold Sicilian spoon dessert of ice crystals, often flavored with fruits. This particular version, however, is primarily associated with Messina, where it is served alongside brioche for breakfast.

PREPARATION TIME 10 minutes
COOKING TIME 5 minutes
FREEZING TIME 2 hours
SERVES 6

5 ounces/⅔ cup/140 g superfine (caster) sugar
50 fl oz/6¼ cups/1.5 litres extra strong coffee
8 fl oz/1 cup/250 ml whipping cream or heavy (double) cream (optional)

Place the sugar in a large saucepan, add 17 fl oz/2 cups/ 500 ml water, and heat over a low heat until the sugar has dissolved. Add the coffee, stir, and set aside until completely cooled.

Pour the mixture into a large freezerproof container and place in the freezer for 2 hours or just over, stirring every 20 minutes to give it a granular texture.

Just before serving, whip the cream in a large bowl with an electric whisk to soft peaks or use a stand mixer fitted with a whisk attachment. Serve the granita in dishes or glasses and top with whipped cream, if desired.

Sardinia

From malloreddus to porceddu

If the color of Sardinia is the turquoise-green of the sea, its flavor is that of the bittersweet mirto, the iconic liqueur made from purple berries of the myrtle bushes that grow wild all over the island. There is an ancient and still authentic Sardinia that makes a simple meal of bread and cheese—but what breads and what cheeses! Both are made in the finest artisan tradition, and once you start, it is hard to stop cutting slices of Fiore Sardo, a still-young pecorino cheese that has already developed an alluring flavor and which marries wonderfully with the fruitiness of white Vermentino di Gallura wine. And if Fiore Sardo is semi-matured, its crumbly, fatty, and slightly grainy consistency is better paired with a glass of red Cannonau wine.

In Sardinia, the sweetness of the lobster (page 327) will enchant your palate for life. Yet there is so much more than the beauty of its coastline and sea. There is also the beauty of the produce grown on the land, such as the durum wheat used to make pasta, and the beauty of a cuisine that shows respect for the original flavor of meat— the kid goat, mutton, lamb (pages 328 and 330), and porceddu, suckling pig. Finally, the delicious honeys capture the fragrance of every flower, including sulla and asphodel.

Flatbread with tomato sauce

Pane frattau

A simple Sardinian dish. The base ingredient is pane carasau, a crispy flatbread typical of the region, which is dipped quickly in stock to prevent it becoming soggy, and topped with tomato sauce and a poached egg.

PREPARATION TIME 10 minutes
COOKING TIME 15 minutes
SERVES 4

Vegetable stock, for dipping
3 sheets pane carasau (Sardinian crispy flatbread), cut into
  large pieces
14 ounces/1.5 cups/400 g tomato sauce
Pecorino cheese, grated, for sprinkling
1 egg
Salt and black pepper
Extra-virgin olive oil

Heat some stock in a large saucepan, then dip the pieces of bread into it, one at a time. Do this very quickly to wet the bread without soaking it.

Lay three pieces of bread in a large serving dish and cover with plenty of tomato sauce, then cover the sauce with a layer of cheese and three more pieces of bread. Repeat the process to make two more layers. This recipe is limited to three layers, but as there is no rule for this, you can continue as you please, judging by the number of diners.

Bring a medium saucepan of water to a boil. Once boiling, using a whisk or the handle of a wooden spoon, swirl the water to create a whirlpool in the center of the pan, then break the egg into the middle and cook for 4 minutes, or until the white is set. Using a skimmer, carefully lift out the egg and place on top of the last layer of the bread. Serve.

Fregula with seafood

Fregula is a dried pasta that is prepared throughout
Sardinia and flavored in many ways. Here, the fregula
is cooked like risotto with the addition of shellfish.
A traditional, tasty, and healthy dish.

PREPARATION TIME 1 hour 10 minutes

COOKING TIME 30 minutes

RESTING TIME 3–12 hours

SERVES 4

1 pound 2 ounces/500 g mussels

2 tablespoons extra-virgin olive oil, plus extra for steaming
  and drizzling

2 cloves garlic, peeled but left whole

Handful of parsley, finely chopped

1 pound 2 ounces/500 g clams

10 fl oz/1¼ cups/300 ml fish stock

5 baby squid, cleaned and cut into strips

1 shallot, finely chopped

1 tablespoon tomato paste (purée)

10½ ounces/2 cups/300 g fregula

1¾ fl oz/scant ¼ cup/50 ml white wine

10½ ounces/300 g small shrimp (prawns), peeled and deveined

Salt and black pepper

Thoroughly clean the mussels. Scrape any debris off the
shells, remove the beards, and wash them well under
cold running water. Discard any broken or empty shells,
then place the intact mussels in a large skillet (frying
pan) with a lid. Add a splash of oil, a garlic clove, and
some parsley. Place over a high heat, cover with a lid,
and wait for the shells to open. Remove and set the
mussels aside, discarding any that remain closed.

To clean the clams, place them in a fine-mesh strainer
(sieve) inside a large bowl or basin filled with cold salted
water and soak them overnight (or for at least 3 hours).
This way, any sand or grit they expel will remain at the
bottom of the bowl or basin.

Drain the clams and rinse them in cold water. Put the clams
in a large skillet (frying pan) with a lid. Add a splash of oil,
the remaining garlic clove, and two-thirds of the parsley,
place over a high heat, cover with a lid, and wait for the

clams to open. Discard any clams that remain closed.
When both the mussels and clams are cooked, drain,
collect and strain their cooking liquor, and pour it into
the fish stock.

Heat the 2 tablespoons oil in a nonstick pan with the
chopped shallot and tomato paste (purée). Add the
fregula and toast as if it were rice, stirring continuously.
Pour in the wine and stir to deglaze the pan, then allow
the alcohol to evaporate. Gradually add the stock, stirring
the pasta occasionally while cooking to stop it from sticking.

Halfway through cooking, add the squid, followed by
the shrimp (prawns), mix, and continue to cook. Shortly
before the end of the cooking time, add the mussels
and clams. Adjust the seasoning with salt and pepper.
Serve with a drizzle of extra-virgin olive oil and a
sprinkle of parsley.

Malloreddus with pecorino

Malloreddus—also known as Sardinian gnocchi—is a traditional durum wheat pasta of the region. Ideally, the cheese used in this recipe should be Pecorino Sardo (PDO), made from the milk of the local sheep, the *Sarda*.

PREPARATION TIME 20 minutes

COOKING TIME 20 minutes

RESTING TIME 30 minutes

SERVES 4

10½ ounces/300 g cherry tomatoes, halved and seeded
1 clove garlic, halved
2 tablespoons olive oil
14 ounces/400 g malloreddus
Fresh oregano leaves, for sprinkling
2 ounces/50 g Pecorino Sardo (PDO), shaved
Salt and black pepper

Place the tomatoes and garlic in a large bowl and mix well. Cover with plastic wrap (cling film) and leave to rest for 30 minutes.

Heat the oil in a large skillet (frying pan), add the cherry tomatoes and garlic, and sauté for a few minutes. Remove the garlic and discard, and season the tomatoes with salt and pepper. Remove from the heat and set aside.

Cook the pasta in a large saucepan of boiling salted water until they float to the top, then drain and add to the pan with the tomatoes. Sauté for 1 minute, then transfer to a serving dish and sprinkle with oregano and cheese. Mix and serve.

Spaghetti with bottarga

A pasta dish with an intense taste of the sea. Bottarga is made by salting and drying the roe produced by the mullet that live in ponds around Cabras, Sardinia. Use the best quality bottarga you can find for this dish.

PREPARATION TIME 15 minutes

COOKING TIME 20 minutes

SERVES 4

11 ounces/320 g spaghetti
2–3 tablespoons olive oil
2 cloves garlic, lightly crushed
1 shallot, finely chopped
3 tablespoons grated mullet bottarga
Mullet bottarga shavings, for sprinkling
Salt

Cook the pasta in a large saucepan of boiling salted water for 10 minutes, or until al dente.

Meanwhile, start to prepare the flavoring. Heat the oil in a skillet (frying pan), add the garlic and shallot, and sauté for a few minutes.

When the pasta is cooked, drain, and set aside some of the cooking water. Add the pasta to the pan with the flavoring and toss briefly until well combined. Sprinkle with some grated bottarga. Stir quickly, adding a little of the cooking water if necessary.

Divide the pasta between individual plates, top with additional bottarga shavings, as desired, and serve immediately.

Catalan-style lobster

Aragosta alla catalana

This dish originated in Alghero in the northwest of the island, evidence of the strong Catalan influence in the city following the arrival of Catalan settlers in the fourteenth century.

PREPARATION TIME 1 hour

COOKING TIME 20 minutes

SERVES 4

2 spiny lobsters, about 1 pound 2 ounces

1 Tropea red onion, sliced into rings

15 cherry tomatoes or 2–3 ripe but firm tomatoes, cut into wedges

Olive oil, for dressing

Lemon juice, for dressing

Salt

FOR A MORE SUBSTANTIAL DISH

2–3 carrots, thinly sliced

1 small head chicory, cut into small pieces

1 head white celery, cut into small pieces

1 scallion (spring onion), white part only, thinly sliced

1 red bell pepper, cored, seeded, and sliced

1 yellow bell pepper, cored, seeded, and sliced

1 bunch radishes, peel decoratively cut into stripes

FOR THE VINAIGRETTE (OPTIONAL)

1¾ fl oz/scant ¼ cup/50 ml extra-virgin olive oil

1 tablespoon white wine vinegar

Juice of 1 lemon

½ teaspoon Dijon mustard

Salt and pepper

Boil the lobsters in a large saucepan of lightly salted water for 15–20 minutes, then drain. Make incisions into the side of the shell, remove the carapace and the central membrane, and set aside any larger claws for another use.

Cut the still-hot tail meat into pieces and arrange it in a serving dish. Add the onion and cherry tomatoes. Dress everything with oil, salt, and lemon juice and serve.

For a more substantial dish, arrange all the ingredients in the serving dish together with the lobster, onion, and tomatoes. Then make the vinaigrette by whisking the oil, vinegar, lemon juice, mustard, and salt and pepper to taste together in a bowl and drizzle it over everything.

Lamb meatballs

Sardinian lamb has PGI status, and is some of the best in Italy. A popular meat served at the Easter table, here it is ground (minced) and served as meatballs in a traditional second course dish.

PREPARATION TIME 30 minutes

COOKING TIME 10 minutes

SERVES 6

3 tablespoons torn stale bread pieces
1 pound 12 ounces/800 g boneless lamb shoulder, ground (minced)
1 egg, beaten
1 small onion, finely chopped
1 clove garlic, finely chopped
2 sprigs mint, finely chopped
4 tablespoons vegetable oil
Salt and black pepper

Blitz the bread in a food processor to crumbs, then add to a bowl, cover with water, and leave to soak for 5 minutes. Once the water has been absorbed, squeeze the crumbs and then crumble into finer crumbs.

Remove any skin and excess fat from the meat, then grind (mince) it in a grinder (mincer). Add it to a large bowl with the bread crumbs, beaten egg, onion, garlic, and mint leaves and mix together. Season with salt and pepper and mix to combine.

Dampen your hands and form the mixture into 18 meatballs. Flatten them slightly.

Heat the oil in a large skillet (frying pan) over a medium heat. Add the meatballs in batches if necessary, and fry for about 5 minutes on each side until browned and cooked through. Remove them with a slotted spoon and drain on paper towels. Arrange the meatballs in a serving dish and serve hot.

Lamb with wild fennel

From spring through summer, the yellow flowers of the wild fennel that grows in abundance across the island are a familiar sight, providing ample opportunity for foraging of this aniseed-flavored herb.

PREPARATION TIME 30 minutes

COOKING TIME 1 hour

SERVES 6

All-purpose (plain) flour, for coating

5 pounds 8 ounces/2.5 kg leg of lamb, cut into pieces

1¾ fl oz/scant ¼ cup/50 ml olive oil

1 onion, chopped

9 ounces/250 g tomatoes, skinned and strained (sieved), or 1 tablespoon tomato paste (purée) diluted with a little warm water

2 pounds 4 ounces/1 kg wild fennel fronds

Salt and black pepper

Spread enough flour for coating the lamb on a large plate. Season the lamb pieces with salt and pepper, then toss in the flour until coated all over.

Heat the oil in a large skillet (frying pan) over medium heat, add the lamb pieces, and brown all over. Add the onion and sauté for 10 minutes, or until golden. Stir in the tomatoes or the diluted tomato paste (purée) and continue to cook over a medium heat.

Meanwhile, fill another pan with 17 fl oz/2 cups/500 ml water, set it over a high heat, add the wild fennel fronds,

and boil for 10 minutes, then drain, setting aside the cooking water.

Add all the fennel cooking water to the pan with the meat, adjust the seasoning with salt and pepper, and cook for 40 minutes. After 30 minutes, add the fennel to the pan.

When cooked, remove the pan from the heat, transfer the stew to a serving dish, and serve.

Saffron and ricotta tartlets

These star-shaped tartlets are a traditional sweet bite in Sardinia. Also known as *casadinas* or *formagelle*, depending on where you are in the region, these are part tartlet, part cake, and totally delicious.

PREPARATION TIME 30 minutes
COOKING TIME 30 minutes
RESTING TIME 30 minutes
SERVES 6

10½ ounces/2½ cups/300 g all-purpose (plain) flour, plus extra
    for dusting
1 tablespoon lard
1 tablespoon unsalted butter, softened
2 eggs
Salt

FOR THE FILLING
1 sachet saffron threads
Milk, for diluting the saffron
10½ ounces/1¼ cups/300 g ewe's milk ricotta cheese
5½ ounces/⅔ cup/150 g superfine (caster) sugar
Grated zest of ½ orange
Grated zest of ½ lemon

To make the dough, mix 9 ounces/2 cups/250 g of the flour, the lard, butter, eggs, and a pinch of salt together in a large bowl. Knead the dough vigorously for a few minutes, then wrap it in plastic wrap (cling film) and refrigerate for 30 minutes.

For the filling, place the saffron threads in a small bowl and cover with a little milk. Add the ricotta to a large bowl, then add the sugar, grated orange and lemon zests, and saffron with milk, and mix and knead until the mixture is very firm.

Preheat the oven to 350 °F/180 °C/160 °Cfan/Gas 4. Line a large baking sheet with parchment paper.

Roll the dough out on a lightly floured work surface until it is ¼ inch/5 mm thick. Using a pastry cutter, cut out 3¼–4-inch/8–10-cm disks. Pinch the edges of each disk at regular intervals so that they resemble small bowls. Arrange them on the prepared baking sheet and fill them with the ricotta mixture.

Bake in the preheated oven for about 30 minutes, until the crust is golden. Remove from the oven and set aside to cool to room temperature before serving.

Honey and cheese pastries

A quintessential Sardinian dessert, these mini parcels are a mix of sweet and savory—a beautiful flaky pastry dumpling filled with citrus-scented cheese, sprinkled with sugar, and dipped in honey.

PREPARATION TIME 20 minutes

COOKING TIME 30 minutes

RESTING TIME 30 minutes

SERVES 6

FOR THE PASTRY
10½ ounces/2½ cups/300 g all-purpose (plain) flour, plus extra
  for dusting
2 ounces/generous ¼ cup/50 g lard
1 tablespoon olive oil

FOR THE FILLING
10½ ounces/300 g fresh pecorino cheese, shaved
2 teaspoons superfine (caster) sugar
2 teaspoons ground cinnamon
Grated zest of 1 lemon or orange

TO FINISH
Vegetable oil, for deep-frying
Superfine (caster) sugar, for sprinkling
Orange blossom honey or bitter honey, for dipping

For the pastry, place the flour, lard, oil, and as much water as necessary to obtain a smooth and soft dough in a large bowl and mix together. Gather the dough into a ball, cover with plastic wrap (cling film), and leave it to rest for 30 minutes.

Roll out the pastry on a lightly floured work surface and cut out many small disks of your preferred size. Top each disk with one or two pecorino cheese shavings, and a little sugar, cinnamon, and grated citrus zest. Fold the pastries over and seal the edges well.

Heat plenty of vegetable oil in a large skillet (frying pan), add the pastries in batches, and fry until they turn golden brown. Remove with a slotted spoon, shake off the oil, and drain on paper towels. Sprinkle the pastries with sugar, dip them quickly in honey, arrange them on a serving plate, and serve immediately.

Index

Recipe notes

Butter should always be unsalted, unless otherwise specified. All herbs are fresh, unless otherwise specified.

Eggs are large (UK medium), unless otherwise specified.

Individual vegetables and fruits, such as onions and apples, are assumed to be medium, unless otherwise specified.

All milk is whole (3% fat), homogenized, and lightly pasteurized, unless otherwise specified.

Salt is always kosher salt, unless otherwise specified.

Exercise a high level of caution when following recipes involving any potentially hazardous activity, including the use of high temperatures, open flames and when deep-frying. In particular, when deep-frying add food carefully to avoid splashing, wear long sleeves and never leave the pan unattended.

Cooking times are for guidance only. If using a fan (convection) oven, follow the manufacturer's instructions concerning the oven temperatures.

All herbs, shoots, flowers and leaves should be picked fresh from a clean source. Do exercise caution when foraging for ingredients, which should only be eaten if an expert has deemed them safe to eat. In particular, do not gather wild mushrooms yourself before seeking the advice of an expert who has confirmed their suitability for human consumption. As some species of mushrooms have been known to cause allergic reaction and illness, do take extra care when cooking and eating mushrooms and do seek immediate medical help if you experience a reaction after preparing or eating them.

Exercise caution when making fermented products, ensuring all equipment is spotlessly clean, and seek expert advice if in any doubt.

When no quantity is specified, for example of oils, salts and herbs used for finishing dishes, quantities are discretionary and flexible.

All spoon and cup measurements are level, unless otherwise stated. 1 teaspoon = 5 ml; 1 tablespoon = 15 ml. Australian standard tablespoons are 20 ml, so Australian readers are advised to use 3 teaspoons in place of 1 tablespoon when measuring small quantities.

Cup, metric and imperial measurements are used in this book. Follow one set of measurements throughout, not a mixture, as they are not interchangeable.

Phaidon Press Limited
2 Cooperage Yard
London E15 2QR

Phaidon Press Inc.
111 Broadway
New York, NY 10006

phaidon.com

First published 2025
©2025 Phaidon Press Limited

The recipes in this book are adapted from various publications in The Silver Spoon family including *Cucina regionale*. The first English edition of *The Silver Spoon* was published by Phaidon in 2005. First published in Italian by Editoriale Domus as *Il cucchiaio d'argento* 1950. Tenth edition (revised, expanded, and redesigned) 2016. © Editoriale Domus

ISBN – 978 0 7148 4921 8

A CIP catalogue record for this book is available from the British Library and the Library of Congress.

Printed in China

Commissioning Editor: Emilia Terragni
Project Editor: Rachel Malig
Designer: Lacasta Design
Production Controller: Gary Hayes
Food styling: Ellie Mulligan
Prop styling: Rachel de Vere

All photography by Matt Russell, except:
Simon Bajada: pages 236, 239
Edward Park: pages 146, 161, 300
Alamy Stock Photo, pages: 18 Adam Eastland; 34 Robert Harding; 47 Martina Fassino/Stockimo; 48 Art Kowalsky; 62 Brian Jannsen; 76 Jon Arnold Images Ltd; 91 Farway Photos; 92 imageBROKER.com GmbH & Co. KG; 110 Nicola Simeoni; 126 Stefano Valeri; 143 Frank Chmura; 162 SFM ITALY D; 174 and 187 David Noton Photography; 188 Tristan Deschamps; 206 Corina Daniela Obertas; 220 CF Photos; 222 Robert Wyatt; 254 Michele D'Ottavio; 282 Liane M; 318 Michael Brooks

The publisher would like to thank Evelyn Battaglia, Vanessa Bird, Ayushi Channawar, Lara Cook, Alice Earll, Claudia Gschwend, Hélène Gallois Montbrun, João Mota, Ruth Samuels, Ellie Smith, Tracey Smith, Kathy Steer, and Hans Stofregen for their contributions to the book.